*How Innovation
and Vision Created
a Network Giant*

LARRY MACDONALD

JOHN WILEY & SONS
Toronto • New York • Chichester • Weinheim • Brisbane • Singapore

John Wiley & Sons Canada Ltd
22 Worcester Road
Etobicoke, Ontario
M9W 1L1

Canadian Cataloguing in Publication Data

MacDonald, Larry
  Nortel Networks : how innovation and vision created a network giant

Includes index.
ISBN 0-471-64542-7

1. Nortel Networks – History. 2. Northern Telecom Limited – History. I. Title.

HD9696.T444N67 2000   338.7'621382   C00-932210-8

Production Credits
Cover & Text Design: Interrobang Graphic Design Inc.
Printer: Tri-Graphic Printing

10 9 8 7 6 5 4 3 2 1

To my father and mother

Contents

Acknowledgements

A special thanks to editor Karen Milner, who assisted with the selection of Nortel as the subject of the book, and to editor Ron Edwards, for his astute eye. Also, special thanks to Joy, for her patience and support.

I am indebted to Lawrence Surtees, telecommunication reporter with *The Globe and Mail*. He generously responded to requests for unpublished materials; his articles in *The Globe and Mail* and his book, *Pa Bell: Jean de Grandpré and the Meteoric Rise of Bell Canada Enterprises*, (Toronto: Random House, 1992) were all quite valuable sources of information on Nortel.

Another valuable source was *NORTEL, Northern Telecom: Past, Present, and Future*, (Mississauga: Northern Telecom, 1996), written by Peter Newman. Also useful was material supplied by Professor Leenders and his associates at the Richard Ivey School of Business (located at the University of Western Ontario), as well as other material provided by Charlie Gee.

To all the people interviewed, I would like to thank them for what were very enjoyable and informative sessions. Those interviewed included senior Nortel executives such as John Roth (CEO and president) and Ian Craig (former chief marketing officer), as well as Nortel retirees such as Colin Beaumont (former chief engineer), Rudolph Kriegler (former vice president of technology), Peter Cashin (former assistant vice president of computing research), and Helmuth Krausbar (former project manager on the hardware side of digital switches).

A Brief History of Nortel Networks

Note: All dollar figures in book are in U.S. currency unless otherwise stated.

1876   Alexander Graham Bell obtains U.S. Patent No. 174465 for invention of telephone.

1880   Bell Telephone Company of Canada (predecessor to Bell Canada, the future parent company of Nortel Networks) is formed in Montreal, Quebec.

1882   Bell Telephone Company of Canada creates the Mechanical Department to manufacture telephone sets.

1886   Manufacturing of telephone switchboards (the 50-line Standard Magneto Switchboard) commences.

1895   Bell Telephone Company of Canada spins off its manufacturing operations into a separate corporation called Northern Electric and Manufacturing Company (forerunner to Nortel Networks); expands manufacturing of non-telephone product lines, including fire alarm boxes and sleigh bells.

1900   Northern Electric and Manufacturing Company produces the first phonographs in Canada for Emile Berliner, inventor of the flat-disc phonograph.

1907   First sales office set up in Winnipeg, Manitoba.

1913   Northern Electric and Manufacturing Company signs an agreement with Western Electric governing reciprocal purchases and exchange of patents; relationship continues until 1962.

1914   Northern Electric and Manufacturing Company amalgamates with Imperial Wire & Cable Company to form the Northern Electric Company Limited (owned 44 percent by Western Electric Company, 50 percent by Bell Telephone Company of Canada, and 6.4 percent by others).

1915   Beginning in early 1915, manufacturing plants are converted to military production; output of shells reaches 12,000 per week before the end of war.

1922   Production of first vacuum tube (used as repeater devices on long distance lines) in Canada; manufacturing of consumer radios begins; radio station set up to encourage purchase of radios.

1924   The first automatic telephone exchange on the Bell Canada network installed at the Grover Exchange in Toronto (brings dial sets to Canadian telephone users).

1929   Bell's ownership becomes 56.3 percent; Western Electric's 43.6 percent, and others, 0.01 percent.

1932   Obtains a loan from Western Electric to survive Great Depression.

1933   Nearly 80 percent of workforce (from 1929 peak) have been laid off.

1935   Establishes Dominion Sound Equipment, a wholly owned subsidiary to supply sound equipment to movie theaters.

1940   Manufacturing plants turned over to war effort; produce over 5 million shells and 130,000 feet of mine sweeping cable.

1941   Begins production, under top-secret conditions, of the Magnetron tube (an essential component in radar systems).

1945   Begins broadcast of The Northern Electric Hour on 33 radio stations across Canada.

1946   Introduces Baby Champ table radio; produces mobile radio communications system for Canadian Pacific Railway; construction of Lachine, Quebec, plant for manufacture of wire and cable.

1947   Construction of Belleville, Ontario, plant to manufacture electronic switchboard and key equipment.

1953   Introduction of the Northern Electric tabletop television set, with an RCA picture tube.

1956   January 24, 1956, signing of Consent Decree between AT&T and U.S. Justice Department, which leads to divestiture of Northern Electric from Western Electric.

1957   Sells off radio, TV, and household appliance distribution businesses.

1959   Northern Electric Laboratories organized to coordinate company activities in telecommunications research and development; disposes of theater sound equipment.

1960   London, Ontario, plant opens for manufacturing of telephone sets.

1962   Northern Electric Company Limited becomes a wholly owned subsidiary of Bell Canada.

1963   Plant opens in Brampton, Ontario, to manufacture central office switching systems.

1965   Establishes Advanced Devices Center in Ottawa for the manufacture of transistors and integrated circuits.

1966   Construction begins for new plants in Saint John, New Brunswick, and in Calgary, Alberta; Contempra "dial-in-handset" telephone is demonstrated.

1968   Carterfone decision opens interconnect market in U.S. to competition.

1969   The Advanced Devices Center is incorporated as Microsystems International Ltd., a wholly owned subsidiary.

1970   Northern Electric Laboratories become Bell-Northern Research (BNR) Ltd., jointly owned by Bell Canada and Northern Electric; Northern Telecom (NTI) Inc., is incorporated as a wholly owned subsidiary to manufacture and sell telecommunications equipment in the United States (initially headquartered in Boston but moved to Nashville in 1976).

1972   Opening of first NTI manufacturing plant (in Port Huron, Michigan) to manufacture telephone sets; plant established in Malaysia; the Anik 1 communications satellite, containing a Northern Electric electronic platform, is launched.

1973   Formation of Northern Electric (Europe); construction begins on manufacturing plants in Butner, North Carolina, and Mountain View, California; initial public offering of common shares.

1975   New products include the SL-1 (a digital PBX switch) and the SL-10 (a data network switch); research centers established in Montreal, Quebec, and Palo Alto, California; UK subsidiary and Northern Electric Export Corporation set up.

1976   Northern Electric changes name to Northern Telecom Limited; becomes first company to announce a complete line of fully digital telecommunication switches (the DMS-10 to DMS-350 models); Digital World seminar held at Disney Land.

1977   Sells satellite business; one-millionth SL-1 line put into service (in Cooksville, Ontario); first DMS-10 in service (in Fort White, Florida); construction begins on manufacturing plant in Santa Clara, California.

1978   SL-10 datapac system selling well in Europe; Northern Telecom International Ltd. established to oversee all marketing and manufacturing operations in all markets outside North America.

1979   First DMS-100 service set up (in Ottawa, Ontario); AT&T recommends DMS-10 for use within the Bell System; new feature for SL-1 enables simultaneous handling of voice and data over same wiring (first of its kind).

1980   Moves corporate headquarters from Montreal, Quebec, to Mississauga, Ontario (later, in 1990s, moves headquarters to refurbished Brampton plant near Toronto, Ontario); opening of plant in Research Triangle Park (RTP) near Raleigh/Durham in North Carolina; as demand for Northern Telecom digital switching products mounts in the U.S. in the 1980s, RTP expands into a campus of 17 buildings.

1981   More sales of DMS switches (for example, the U.S. Air Force awards Northern Telecom a contract for 29 DMS-100s); introduction of Displayphone, an "integrated voice/data terminal," which combines a telephone handset, computer terminal, and keyboard, all in one unit.

1982   Wins supply agreement with AT&T for DMS-200 toll switches; announces Open Protocol Enhanced Networks (OPEN) World, a commitment to develop products and services that will provide connectivity and compatibility with a wide variety of products and standards (allowing an organization to manage its data, voice, text, and image messages as one integrated system); General Electric Company and Northern Telecom announce plans to develop, manufacture, and market cellular mobile telephone systems (based on Northern Telecom's switches).

1983   Mitsui & Co., Ltd. signs agreement to distribute the SL-1 in Japan; MCI signs supply agreement for 62,000 miles of fiber-optic cable; Southern Bell signs a four-year supply contract for DMS-100/200 switching systems; Bell Canada Enterprises (BCE) created as a holding company to hold Bell Canada and Northern Telecom (BCE owns 53.4 percent).

1984   Bell operating companies complete break from AT&T and are free to buy equipment from companies other than Western Electric; Northern Telecom signs multiyear supply agreements with several of them, including Ameritech Services Inc. and Pacific Bell; receives order for 60,000 telephone sets from Nippon Telegraph and

Telephone (NTT) in Japan; the Vienna Family of computers and office information systems for the European market are developed and introduced.

1985   The first major contract awarded by NTT to a non-Japanese company is for $250 million of Northern Telecom switching equipment; stream of DMS contracts continue, including BellSouth's four-year $300 million supply contract, GTE Sprint's deal for DMS-300 international gateway switches, and Southwestern Bell's two-year, $300 million supply contract for DMS switching systems; as part of OPEN World strategy, introduces Meridian line of PBXs (integrating voice and data networks in the office).

1986   Digital switch line continues to sell well; examples of business won include the DMS-250 and DMS-300 switches sold to Mercury Communications Limited in the UK, the installation of the Meridian SL-1 system for the Paris Stock Exchange, a $250 million supply agreement for DMS-10 switching systems for the Japanese public network, a $32 million contract with the U.S. Army for Meridian SL-1, and SL-100 systems; by 1986, Northern Telecom has installed five-million SL-1 lines and 1,000 DMS-100 switches.

1987   Buys a minority stake in STC PLC, a leading British supplier of communications and information systems; Vision 2000 outlined (goal to become leading telecom equipment supplier by 2000); introduction of DMS SuperNode (substantial upgrade to DMS-100); a Northern Telecom installation team sets an industry record of only 15 days for the installation of an 18,000-line DMS-100 system in Brooklyn, New York.

1988   Expands Advanced Semiconductor Technology Centre in Ottawa; launches very successful Norstar (an advanced key telephone system for small and medium-sized companies); British Telecom selects STC PLC, in cooperation with Northern Telecom, to supply approximately $170 million of business communications equipment; creates a $200 million provision to cover a company restructuring.

1989   FiberWorld announcement (making Northern Telecom the first telecommunications supplier to commit to providing a fiber-optics network that adheres to international SONET standards); the Society for Worldwide Interbank Financial Telecommunications (SWIFT) signs a $15 million contract for DPN systems to link bank locations in more than 60 countries; delivers one-thousandth data packet switch, a DPN-100, to the U.S. Federal Reserve System.

1990   Northern Telecom acquires more STC PLC shares; starts $100 million expansion of BNR's Lab in Ottawa; SITA, the air transport industry's global telecommunications organization, signs $50 million DPN contract; Sprint announces its Virtual Private Network, a global network powered by DMS-250 switching systems.

1991   Completes acquisition of STC PLC, creating the fourth-largest telecommunications supplier in the world; start of a wireless equipment division under Roth; wins long-term switching contract (worth $200 million) with Telecom Australia; Ameritech signs a switching equipment supply agreement worth an estimated $700 million; Southwestern Bell agrees to a $130 million upgrade its switching equipment.

1992   Northern Telecom and Motorola form a joint venture (later reversed in part) to develop and sell cellular telephone networks; NT CALA formed to market products in the Caribbean and Latin America; Northern Telecom and Matra of France form a strategic alliance covering PBX and GSM products; Bell Canada signs a $900 million switching contract; MCI signs $225 million supply agreement to upgrade its switching equipment and a $250 million agreement for FiberWorld equipment; STC Submarine Systems wins a $370 million contract for undersea cable linking Canada and Europe.

1993   People's Republic of China purchases more than $250 million in DMS equipment; Nortel wins $270 million contract for DMS systems from NTT Japan; Pacific Bell names Northern Telecom as a primary vendor in a five-year, $650 million project; installs 10 millionth line of DMS-10 switching equipment; reports $1 billion loss in second quarter (to cover upgrading of central office switches and corporate restructuring).

1994   Round of asset sales, including STC Submarine Systems and U.S. finance subsidiary; targets expansion into Asia by forming Nortel China; opens new plant in Monterey, Mexico; a second R&D facility established at Harlow, England; beginning of reorganization under COO Roth; end of preferred supplier arrangement with Bell Canada.

1995   Northern Telecom celebrates its 100th anniversary; announces "A World of Networks," a vision in which converged networks figure prominently; announces several alliances including those with Hewlett-Packard, QUALCOMM, Fore Systems, and Cabletron; begins technical trials of the Cornerstone product line for telephone service over cable TV lines; lands several contracts for PCS wireless equipment, including those from BellSouth and GO Communications.

1996   Industry Week magazine selects Northern Telecom as one of the world's 100 Best-Managed Companies; breakthrough $1 billion wireless contract with Sprint; Southwestern Bell becomes first public carrier in the world to deploy Northern Telecom's Internet Thruway (which reduces the cost of handling the explosive growth of Internet traffic); leads the market in commercial deployment of 10 gigabits-per-second fiber-optic networks, with OC-192 systems shipped to Touch America, WorldCom and MCI.

1997   Northern Telecom listed among the Business Week Fifty top performers; Webtone vision articulated (which aims to make the Internet as reliable, available, and secure as the telephone system); Qwest Communications agrees to purchase up to $150 million of fiber-optic transmission equipment to create a 13,000-mile network (the first coast-to-coast OC-192 network) and Williams Communications Group announces a $300 million agreement to build a new coast-to-coast multimedia backbone network, using Northern Telecom's OC-48 and OC-192 and related equipment.

1998   Announces name change, to Nortel Networks Corp. (formally occurs in 1999); multibillion-dollar acquisition of Bay Networks marks right-angle turn into Internet Protocol (IP) networks; acquires the remaining shares of Nortel Technology Limited (formerly BNR) from Bell Canada and initiates integration with business units; market researchers rank Nortel Networks Passport product portfolio number one in global market share; 1-Meg modem sales top $1 billion after only eight months on market.

1999   More than 75 percent of all backbone Internet traffic in North America is carried on Nortel Networks optical equipment; as part of right-angle turn to the Internet, Nortel Networks acquires a series of companies including Shasta Networks (service-enabling gateways at the "subscriber edge" of IP networks), Periphonics, (a leading global provider of interactive voice solutions used in call centers and other voice and data network applications), and Clarify Inc. (the world's second largest provider of front office solutions for e-business); announces agreements with five manufacturing companies to divest and/or outsource certain manufacturing and repair operations.

2000   Allocates hundreds of millions of dollars to expand optical manufacturing capacity; consolidates optical networking units under one roof (called High Performance Optical Components Solutions); continues one-a-month acquisitions spree (taking over Internet-related companies such as Promatory, Clarify, and Xros); wins multi-billion-dollar optical networking contracts from Worldcom Inc., Williams Communications Group and others; BCE divests its Nortel stake, making Nortel an independent company for the first time in its history.

A History of Name Changes for Nortel Networks

1882   The Mechanical Department is set up within Bell Telephone of Canada to manufacture telephone equipment.

1895   Bell Telephone of Canada incorporates its manufacturing department under the name of Northern Electric and Manufacturing Company.

1914   Name changed to The Northern Electric Company Limited after merger with Imperial Wire and Cable Company limited.

1976   Name changed to Northern Telecom Limited as company moves into digital technology.

1995   In the company's hundredth year, the Nortel name is introduced along with a corporate vision outlining a world of converged voice, data, and video networks.

1999   Nortel Networks Corp. becomes the legal name of the company.

Key Executives in the History of Nortel Networks

C. F. Sise Sr.:
    President   1895-1913
    Chairman   1914-1917

Edward F. Sise:
    President   1913-1919

Paul F. Sise:
    President   1919-1948
    Chairman   1948-1951

R. Dickson Harkness:
    President   1948-1961
    Chairman   1961-1962

R. Holley Keefler:
    President   1961-1967
    Chairman   1963-1970

Vernon O. Marquez:
President	1967-1971
CEO	1970-1973
Chairman	1970-1973

John C. Lobb:
President	1971-1974
CEO	1973-1976
Chairman	1974-1976

Robert C. Scrivener:
Chairman	1976-1979
CEO	1976-1979

Walter F. Light:
President	1974-1982
CEO	1979-1984
Chairman	1982-1985

Jean de Grandpré:
Chairman	1980-1982

Edmund Fitzgerald:
President	1982-1985
CEO	1985-1989
Chairman	1985-1990

David Vice:
President	1985-1990

Paul Stern:
CEO	1989-1993
President	1990-1992
Chairman	1990-1993

Jean C. Monty:
CEO	1993-1997
President	1992-1997

O. Bradford Butler:
Chairman	1993-1994

Donald J. Schuenke:
    Chairman   1994-1999

John A. Roth:
    CEO   1997-present
    President   1997-1998
                                              and 1999-present

David House:
    President   1998-1999

Frank Carlucci:
    Chairman   1999-present

Introduction

The Battle to Build the Internet

Nortel turned 100 in 1995. To celebrate, company officials organized a black-tie gala event in Montreal on the evening of April 27. About 800 customers, managers, and employees attended a reception and a Céline Dion concert at the Bell Amphitheater. Amid the clink of wine glasses and buzz of conversation there were peals of laughter. The mood was relaxed and jovial as the pressures of the business world were left behind.

While the past 100 years were certainly worth commemorating, the talk at the gala event was more about the future. The annual report released for the annual meeting held earlier in the day had outlined a new corporate vision called "A World of Networks." This vision recognized that customers in the telecommunication industry wanted more than boxes. They wanted a broad range of solutions for a rapidly evolving world in which voice, data, and video networks were experiencing convergence. It was a vision that formally acknowledged the company's transition from being a supplier of mainly telephone networks to being a supplier of all varieties of networks.

The year 1995 was a milestone for the telecommunication industry as well. That was when the *Telecommunications Act* wound its way through the US Congress and later became law in early 1996. The bill brought about sweeping deregulation of large portions of the telecommunication sector. The local telephone and cable TV markets joined the previously deregulated long-distance telephone market in allowing unrestricted entry and competition. This would create an even greater free-for-all among service providers. It would lead to a greatly expanded war zone in which the only sure winners appeared to be the arms merchants, companies like Nortel that would be selling equipment to the new entrants as well as to the incumbents who had to upgrade their systems to remain competitive.

But with opportunity came danger—new and stronger opponents for Nortel. The *Telecommunications Act* prompted AT&T to divest itself of its equipment-manufacturing arm (which was known for most of its existence as Western Electric). A main reason was that the regional Bell telephone companies, which had been purchasers of equipment from AT&T's manufacturing operations, would not want to continue buying equipment once AT&T became their direct competitor in the deregulated local telephone market. The *Telecommunications Act* hence made it necessary for AT&T to split off its manufacturing arm from its carrier service operations, setting loose a telecommunication Godzilla approximately twice the size of Nortel.

The spin-off started in the fall of 1995 when the manufacturing operations were incorporated as a separate company called Lucent Technologies Inc. In early 1996, 112 million shares of Lucent, representing about 18 percent of the value of the company, were sold at a price of $27 on US exchanges to the public. Underwritten by Morgan Stanley & Co., proceeds were $3 billion—the largest initial public offering up to that time. Another 524 million shares in Lucent, representing the remaining 82 percent value of the company, were issued in September 1996 to AT&T shareholders.

Partly for the same reason, Nortel itself was later set free from its parent company, Bell Canada Enterprises (BCE) Inc. (the successor to central Canada's telephone service provider, Bell Canada Inc.). In May 2000, BCE distributed all but 2 percent of its 37 percent stake in Nortel to BCE stockholders. Nortel would now have more freedom to win business from BCE rivals and pursue its own policies, such as an aggressive acquisitions program.

The deregulated telecommunication markets saw another formidable rival come forward to challenge both Nortel and Lucent—Cisco Systems Inc. Founded in 1984, Cisco has been on a steep growth trajectory ever since, marching past $10 billion in annual sales in less than fifteen years. Its stellar success was based on a line of router products used for directing traffic over data networks. Cisco currently has a market share close to 80 percent—a dominance that makes it the King Kong of data communication.

By the end of this decade, it is expected that networks carrying voice, data, and video signals will have largely converged over packet-based data networks. These networks break various kinds of media into tiny data packets and shoot them in intermingled fashion down a labyrinth of channels around the globe. Routers read headers in each packet to guide them along to their correct destinations, where the disparate pieces of each message are reassembled for the intended listener or viewer.

The chief executive of Cisco, John Chambers, has taken to calling his firm a "New World" company and telecommunication equipment firms "Old World" companies. According to his dichotomy, New World companies have the necessary expertise in data packet networks, move faster, and are more entrepreneurial. By contrast, Old World companies have expertise in outmoded voice-based networks, move slower, and are less responsive to customer needs.

Nortel's chief executive, John Roth, has outlined a countervailing vision, which he calls Webtone. This vision acknowledges that the world of networks is moving to convergence, but he points out that data networks still have quite a way to go before they are as fast, reliable, and secure as telephone networks. Indeed, heading into the 2000s, most voice transmissions now occurring over Internet Protocol (IP) data networks are still low quality. They tend to be choppy and encounter delays in transmission because some of the data packets get left behind in the transmission channel. Nortel's goal is to lead the way to converged networks that are up to the same high standards as the telephone system. In stump speeches, Roth likes to reinforce this point by saying he "can learn to spell IP faster than Cisco can learn to spell reliable." [1]

Recognizing the looming clash of the titans, Chambers approached both Nortel and Lucent in early 1997 with proposals to adopt a cooperative approach to exploiting the immense commercial opportunities inherent in building the Internet infrastructure. These talks smacked of collusion, and, indeed, the US Federal Trade Commission (FTC) later sent letters of inquiry to all three. When he received his letter, Chambers stated there was no intention to violate antitrust laws, nor was there any attempt to hide the discussions—they were publicized in several industry forums beforehand.

In any event, nothing came of the discussions; the main problem was that the product portfolios of the three titans were too large and overlapping. For any company to exit a particular segment would entail a substantial sacrifice of revenues. Nor was it likely that they could have set up joint ventures on selected product lines while competing on others.

Since then, the gloves have come off, as highlighted by a flurry of acquisitions aimed at entering each other's strongholds. Nortel, for example, paid over $7 billion in 1998 to acquire Bay Networks, a Cisco rival in the data networking industry. Nearly a year later, Lucent purchased the second-largest data networking firm, Ascend Communications for $20 billion. For its part, Cisco has spent several billion dollars for firms such as Cerent Corp. to gain admission into the sizzling fiber-optic segment of telecommunication.

Senior executives are engaging in the kind of posturing and banter that often precedes a boxing match. The feud between Lucent and Cisco appears to be the most acrimonious, having spilled over into the courts (Lucent sued Cisco for patent infringement, while Cisco retaliated with a countersuit). Lucent's chief executive, Richard McGinn, put up wanted posters of Chambers and Roth on Lucent premises as a way to whip up the troops. Another Lucent executive taunted Cisco with getting in over its head: "Cisco is coming to play on our turf. This space is bigger than anything Cisco has ever been involved in," he said. [2]

All three companies are allocating substantial research and development resources to addressing quality of service issues surrounding data networks. Cisco is working on software that will make routers more intelligent—that is, able to distinguish between different kinds of packet traffic, give priority to time-sensitive transmissions. That way, voice messages will be sent through immediately without lag or interruption, while transmissions of media less sensitive to time, such as e-mail, are sent later if there is congestion.

Nortel and Lucent are working on alternative approaches of combining voice and data on networks. Nortel's Succession strategy for telephone carriers with legacy systems, for example, redirects data traffic off their circuit-based telephone networks onto data packet overlays, retaining voice transmissions over the telephone network. This is a less-expensive solution that retains voice quality while keeping the telephone network from being overloaded by the escalation in data traffic brought on by the Internet, fax machines, and other sources. It helps the carrier make the transition to an IP world in a more evolutionary way than what Cisco is proposing.

In the meantime, Nortel is looking at reducing the appeal of Cisco's proprietary routers by slashing the prices of its own routers (obtained from Bay Networks) and licensing the underlying software to hundreds of providers of household appliances and other devices that will increasingly connect to the Internet. This shot directed at Cisco represents an attempt to commoditize the router market by pushing the underlying intelligent features of a router off onto third-party servers and related equipment.

All three combatants are also allocating substantial resources to a second front in the battle: the fiber-optic systems that will enable carriers to expand the transmission capacity of the Internet. Cisco has come only recently to the field and is moving to build a presence by cobbling together a number of acquisitions of fiber-optic companies. Nortel and Lucent have research and development programs extending back at least two decades and are augmenting their positions further with fiber-optic acquisitions of their own.

Although Nortel was not involved in most of the original fiber-optic breakthroughs, it was able to bring many of them to commercial application quicker than other companies. As a result, 75 percent of Internet traffic in North America traveled through Nortel's pipes in 1999, which places the company at the very heart of the Internet. Its OC-192 system, based on ten-gigabit-per-second technology, was the most advanced in terms of transmission speed and affordability.

In early 2000, Nortel's fiber-optic systems were capable of transporting the entire contents of the Library of Congress (four million books) from coast to coast in fourteen seconds. In years ahead, this will get down to fractions of a second as Nortel proceeds down its version of Moore's Law. The latter, originated by one of the founders of Intel, foresaw that the technological capacity of semiconductor chips would double every eighteen months. Nortel's version anticipates transmission capacity will double every nine months.

A third front on which all three networking giants are focused is the wireless Internet, said to be the next great inflection point in the networking industry. According to market research firms Yankee Group and Herschel Shosteck Associates, in terms of preparing to build these new networks, Cisco and Lucent take a backseat to Nortel. They rate Nortel number one overall for positioning to roll out the wireless Internet.

In short, Nortel is at the forefront of laying down the information superhighways now revolutionizing the lives of everybody everywhere. Indeed, Nortel has a good shot at becoming the number-one provider of Internet infrastructure, of becoming a Microsoft or Intel for the 2000s. This book, in providing a look at the emergence and prospects for Nortel, is, in part, an introduction to one of the biggest stories now unfolding: the fierce rivalry of three titans to construct and expand the networks of the future.

⌗

It is somewhat remarkable that a centenarian company is at the center of rolling out the Internet. Many companies come and go in the ever-changing technology industries. They burn brightly for a time following the launch of an exciting new product, but then they fade away when another company leapfrogs ahead on the technology curve. Nortel is one of the exceptions. The company has experienced many ups and downs over the years, but it has somehow managed to make vital transitions from old to new technologies.

To keep the image of the company current with evolving technological trends, there have been several name changes along the way. The first name, starting in 1895, was Northern Electric and Manufacturing Company. Under this label, the company was at the forefront of bringing the technology of an earlier era—the telephone, fire alarm boxes, phonographs, and other electrical appliances—to the population in its home base of Canada. In the middle of the 1970s, the company's name was changed to Northern Telecom Limited to reflect the change in its product portfolio arising from new telecommunication services such as data transmissions. The third name change, to Nortel Networks Corp., came near the end of the 1990s to acknowledge the growth and convergence of global networks for voice, data, and video transmission.

The past four decades have been the most remarkable phase for this centenarian of technology companies, as indicated by virtually uninterrupted growth in annual revenues from approximately $200 million in the early 1960s to $22 billion in 1999. In the process, its common shares, first listed in 1973 on the Toronto Stock Exchange (and a few years later on the New York, London, and Tokyo exchanges), have made long-term investors very wealthy. The first ten years of trading, to 1983, brought an appreciation of over 1,000 percent. After a period of drifting in the 1980s, the stock price resumed its upward trend with vigor in the 1990s, although there were some short-term setbacks in 1993 and 1998. The final two years of the decade were especially strong, when the share price quadrupled from the 1998 low. The severe recessions of the early 1980s and 1990s did little to halt the advance; in fact, Nortel shares were one of the few to rise during those troubling times.

Here is a company that appears to be doing something right. How so? How was it able to reinvent itself and adapt to new challenges? What are the lessons for managers, employees, business consultants, and academics? What are the insights for technology investors seeking to spot long-term winners? What are the lessons for economists and policy makers concerned about nurturing key industries and new technologies? These are some of the questions addressed in this book.

One of the main factors in the Nortel success story is capitalizing on discontinuities, those sudden breaks in the environment or the way things are done. They have been what Nortel looks for in order to survive and gain position. When a discontinuity occurs, it is a new race in which all participants go back to the same starting line. Without discontinuities, the advantage would be to the established firm, the one that possesses a dominant share of the market and superior resources. But introduce change—either to the technology or to the market framework itself—and it's a whole new ball game.

The discontinuities that Nortel exploited were, of course, technological—the transition from analog to digital telephone systems, from wired to wireless communications, and from copper-based to fiber-optic transmission systems. The company did not have the depth of the genius of AT&T's Bell Laboratories to come up with basic breakthroughs in technology. But it did have an executive and research team with the foresight and know-how to turn technological breakthroughs into commercial successes faster than others.

In addition to the technological discontinuities, however, there were the discontinuities in the marketplace. These latter disruptions made a significant contribution to the company's progress, on a par with the technological disruptions. It was not one or the other, but a coincidence of both that lifted Nortel upward.

The source of most of the market discontinuities was the deregulation of the telecommunication industry. The framework of government intervention had come about in the early part of the twentieth century because of the assumption that the natural structure of the telephone industry was one of monopoly. As there could really be only one giant telephone network connecting all subscribers together in order for telephone service to be useful, the firm that owned and operated the common carrier would necessarily be a monopoly supplier. Government approval of telephone subscriber rates and prohibitions on the business activities of telephone companies were therefore seen as guarding against the potential abuses of natural monopoly.

In the 1960s, this view of the telephone industry began to change. A major turning point came in 1968 when the US Federal Communication Commission (FCC) ruled in favor of an applicant seeking to attach equipment to the telephone network. This landmark case, known as the *Carterfone* decision, gave customers a choice: they no longer had to lease equipment just from AT&T. They would be able to buy or lease any kind of telephone equipment from any available supplier and be free to plug it into the telephone jack on their premises.

As such, a vast new market was opened up for Nortel and other equipment suppliers. It spurred the very lucrative business communication market: the purchase of on-premise telephone systems known as Private Branch Exchanges (PBXs). The latter were used at first for simply directing incoming calls to various employees within a company, but then later, they evolved to include features such as call forward, call display, and hands-free operation. Other marketable equipment included key telephone systems (eventually integrated with PBXs), which gave a telephone multiple lines in a row of keys or buttons.

Another major change to the US regulatory framework occurred in 1971, when the FCC allowed interconnection to the telephone network. As a result, Microwave Communication Inc. (MCI), which was offering a regional microwave carrier service since obtaining FCC permission in 1969, would be able to hook into the telephone network and compete against AT&T in the market for long-distance calling. Other companies outside of the Bell system were free to enter the common carrier industry as well. This meant that equipment suppliers such as Nortel had an expanding list of customers for telephone infrastructure equipment.

Yet the best was still to come. The biggest market discontinuity lay just ahead in the 1980s—the breakup of the AT&T monopoly following an antitrust investigation by the US Justice Department. Under the court-ordered settlement, AT&T would be limited, as of 1984, to providing long-distance service and to manufacturing telecommunication equipment. The 22 regional Bell companies that had been part of the AT&T empire would be divested and taken over by seven autonomous regional holding companies. The latter would be allowed to supply local telephone service but not long-distance service or to manufacture equipment.

With the bang of the judge's gavel, a vast new market opened up for Nortel, one that would be worth billions of dollars to the company in the 1980s. Severed from their controlling parent, the regional phone companies would be free to purchase equipment from any supplier they wished. Moreover, the number of suppliers competing against Nortel would be held back by the legal restriction placed on the newly independent regional Bell companies not to manufacture equipment.

At the time, Nortel was still a rather small blip on the radar screen, so the Canadian entrant was not yet fully in the sights of AT & T's Western Electric and other US suppliers. On top of this, Nortel was fully prepared for the opportunity. Its full line of digital telephone switches—the only digital versions available anywhere—would be ready just as the market began splitting wide open. As such, it was a wonderful confluence of two discontinuities: one in the marketplace and the other in the technology. Being in the right place at the right time—this is a situation in which Nortel has found itself often throughout its history. It has happened too many times to be happenstance; it would appear to be Nortel's creed.

The theme of exploiting discontinuities is but one of several in this book. Other themes relate to the role of institutional arrangements, such as the important link to a parent corporation and the industrial development policies of the government. Yet other themes relate to the internal dynamics of the corporation—for example, recurring organizational changes, the strategic foresight and vision of senior executives, and the efforts of key individuals who put their heart into their work and sometimes took matters into their own hands. Hopefully there will be lessons in the different themes for all readers.

But Nortel is more than a case study from which to glean lessons. The company is a drama in itself. The enduring and diverse nature of Nortel is a rich tapestry woven from many threads. Moving on and off the stage is a panorama of person-alities, ranging from the crafty to the forceful to the disdained. Some reach pinnacles of wealth and esteem, while others leave under a cloud. Then there are the ups and downs of business life—the times when financial ruin seemed to be around the corner and the times when everything was booming. Finally, intertwined throughout this fabric of people and commerce, is the marvel of technology and its progression—from the dis-covery of how voice vibrations could be carried in the form of analogous electrical waves over telephone wires to the discov-ery of how laser beams flickering several billion times a second can carry a tidal wave of voice, data, and video messages through thin strands of glass fiber.

To fully understand the evolution of Nortel Networks, it is necessary to go back to the beginning. In Chapter 1 the story of Alexander Graham Bell's invention of the telephone in the 1870s provides (aside from some interesting parallels for mod-ern inventors) a brief introduction to how telephone systems function—how handsets convert voice into electrical currents, central offices direct telephone calls, and cables carry electrical signals. Furthermore, the story of the early commercialization of telephone systems provides (aside from some interesting par-allels for modern entrepreneurs) the business context out of which Nortel was to emerge.

1

Good Vibrations

Bell's Phone

The inventor of the telephone, Alexander Graham Bell, came by his interest in sound honestly. His father, Alexander Melville Bell, was a professor of elocution who helped deaf and speech-impaired persons communicate. Bell's grandfather and uncle were also elocutionists. Bell's mother, the daughter of a navy surgeon, was an accomplished musician who went deaf at middle age.

Not surprisingly, Bell followed the family tradition into elocution and speech therapy, although for a time he entertained the idea of becoming a musician. The training received from his father and grandfather was quite extensive, but of particular importance to his future were the lessons on the physiology of how people hear sounds—that is, the mechanics of how the eardrum picks up vibrations in the air and transmits them to the brain so that they can be heard.

Bell was born in Edinburgh, Scotland, on March 3, 1847. Growing up in Scotland, he enjoyed good health throughout his childhood. Then tragedy struck in his early twenties. Bell, along with his two brothers and mother, came down with tuberculosis. After Bell's two brothers died, his father decided to take his wife and remaining son to Canada. He hoped that the change of air would help them recover, just as a sojourn in Newfoundland had helped him recuperate from an illness in his youth.

In the summer of 1870, the Bell family settled near Brantford, Ontario, purchasing a two-story house with a conservatory, stable, and shed located on ten and a half acres of land. During the following autumn, the twenty-four-year-old Alexander Graham Bell lounged in a hammock in the yard, a pale invalid fearing for his life. He did not die. Instead, his chest cleared up, and the energy of life surged back through his veins.

Getting stronger, the ideas began to flow in "this dreaming place," as he called it. His absorbing passion became the application of science to the field of communication. He began to conduct experiments with the objective of inventing devices that would improve the transmission of sound. One was the harmonic telegraph, a new version of the telegraph that would carry more than one message at a time over a wire. Another was the telephone, a term which derives from the Greek roots "tele" (far off) and "phone" (sound).

In 1871, Bell's father received an offer to teach at a school for the deaf in Boston. Already committed to a teaching position at Queen's University in Kingston, Ontario, he passed on the offer to his son. So the young Bell went to the Boston School for the Deaf, where he received an annual salary of $500 as an instructor. While there, a wealthy leather merchant named

Thomas Sanders hired Bell as a private tutor for his deaf son. He was so pleased with the results that he helped finance Bell's spare-time experiments into electrical communication. A Boston lawyer, Gardiner Hubbard, whose daughter was a pupil of Bell's, was also impressed enough with the young man to become a financial backer as well.

In his efforts to help his deaf pupils speak, Bell also worked on developing several mechanical devices. One of them eventually helped lead the way to the invention of the telephone. This was a cardboard tube with a parchment membrane stretched across one end. A sewing needle was attached by a drop of wax to the middle of the membrane, while the other end of the needle rested on a bit of movable smoked glass. Bell discovered that speaking into the tube caused the needle to trace out patterns that were unique to each vowel.

To improve upon this device, he found a Boston doctor who was willing to give him a human ear, which he took back to Brantford on his summer vacation in 1874. Working in his bedroom-study, he secured the ear to a tube with a needle attached to a membrane at the other end. Speaking into the ear, he found he could re-create the unique patterns. At this point, the young Bell had a conceptual revelation: given that different sounds produce specific vibrations, would it not be possible to transmit the human voice over wires by converting the vibrations into electrical impulses?

This conceptual breakthrough was demonstrated about a year later. On his return to Boston, Bell succeeded in convincing Hubbard to pay $9 a week to hire an electrician, Thomas Watson, to assist him. The two men tried several experiments involving tuning forks vibrating in front of iron disks connected to electromagnets. By June 1875, Bell and Watson had abandoned the experiments and were working on the harmonic telegraph project, when Watson tried to loosen a reed too tightly placed against an electromagnet.

The plucking motion transmitted a twanging sound to Bell's room. The inventor rushed excitedly into Watson's room to see what happened. The reed vibrating against the electrical coil had acted like a diaphragm, creating a sound, the timbre of which varied with the intensity of the plucking motion. It was a sign that an electric current, generated by the vibration of an armature in front of an electromagnet, could carry sounds over distance.

Bell and Watson then worked on fashioning a membrane, which, resting on an electromagnet, would transmit sound vibrations over a wire to another electromagnet and membrane device that would re-create the original sound. They succeeded in passing the sound of their voices over the wire, but the words were still indiscernible by the time Bell went back to Brantford on summer vacation.

Feeling confident he was onto something, Bell wrote up the specifications for a patent application at the family home in Brantford. It was filed in the US Patent Office on February 14, 1876, and patent number 174,465, said to be the most lucrative patent ever granted, was allowed on March 3, 1876, the date of Bell's twenty-ninth birthday (and about a year after he had quit his teaching job to work full time on his inventions). Canadian patents followed soon after.

The pressure had been immense. Bell's financial backers were mainly interested in the harmonic telegraph and were after him to get back on track. There were also many persons, including the distinguished Thomas Edison, racing to be the first to develop the telephone. Some of them missed by just days filing for patents ahead of Bell. The disappointed did not give up easily: Bell's patent became the subject of considerable litigation; at various times over the next decade, more than 600 lawsuits were in the courts. The claims were eventually turned away, securing Bell's stature as the father of the telephone.

A few days after the patent was awarded, Bell and Watson were able to transmit the human voice so that the words were discernible. On March 10, 1876, in Boston, Bell called out the historic words, "Mr. Watson, come here. I want you." On hearing the words, Watson came running jubilantly into Bell's room. The words were tinny and faint, but they were nevertheless understandable. More parlor experiments, from one room to the next, were carried out in Boston until the summer break.

Back in Brantford, Bell performed more extensive experiments. He applied for permission to attach his telephones to the telegraph wires of the Dominion Telegraph Company. The manager had at first dismissed Bell as a crank, but the manager's young assistant coaxed his boss to give his consent. In August 1876, Bell successfully demonstrated the transmission of voice over several miles of telegraph wire from a general store to the Bell homestead (the link from the telegraph line on the road into the Bell home was accomplished by stringing stovepipe wire along a fence).

The telephone made Bell famous and rich. Newspapers of the day were full of reports of the wondrous device that transmits the human voice over great distances. Bell won many honors, too. At the Centennial Exhibition in Philadelphia and International Exposition in Paris, held in 1878, he was awarded several medals. Other highlights were the honors received from the government of France, namely the Volta Prize of 50,000 francs and decoration as an Officer of the Legion of Honor.

On July 9, 1877, in Boston, Bell and his two financial backers, Sanders and Hubbard, assigned their jointly owned US patents to a trusteeship, with Hubbard as trustee. Days later, Bell married Mabel, Hubbard's deaf daughter, who had earlier been his pupil. Bell signed over nearly all of his financial interest in the trusteeship to her. Shortly after their marriage, the couple went on a honeymoon to Europe, where he demonstrated the telephone to Queen Victoria.

Bell turned over three-quarters of the Canadian telephone patent to his father, who would be responsible for marketing the telephone invention in Canada. The remaining one-quarter of the patent was assigned to Charles Williams Company, the Boston electrical supply manufacturer that had employed Thomas Watson before Bell. In exchange for the one-quarter ownership, the company pledged to supply 1,000 telephones to Bell's father for distribution to the Canadian market.

In late 1877, Bell and his two backers needed to settle debts run up during the years of research, so they sold their telephone patent and trusteeship to William Forbes and his New England connections. Their remuneration included an equity interest in Forbes' company, which was called National Bell Telephone Company but then later renamed American Bell Telephone Company. The goal of Forbes and his company was to consolidate the fledging US telephone industry through acquisition, litigation, and outmaneuvering the other telephone companies that were just then springing up.

In 1878, the US telegraph giant, Western Union, entered the telephone industry and began to challenge American Bell Telephone Company for supremacy. Western Union hired eminent researchers in the field, particularly Thomas Edison and Elisha Gray, to invent around the Bell patent. They also challenged the validity of the Bell telephone patents in the courts.

Offering their own line of telephone products, Western Union enjoyed considerable success in the early going, and by the end of 1879, the company was operating more than 56,000 telephones in fifty-five US cities.

In 1880, Western Union lawyers advised their management that the Bell patent could not be displaced. This outcome, plus a desire to husband capital for the telegraph side of its business, compelled Western Union to pull the plug on its telephone operations. The company turned over its telephone plant, instruments, and patents to American Bell Telephone Company in exchange for its agreement not to compete in the telegraph industry.

On the news, the price of American Bell Telephone Company stock soared from $50 to $1,000. Since the Bell family and their original financial backers, Sanders and Hubbard, had received shares in the company in remuneration for turning over the telephone patents, the group was catapulted into the ranks of the wealthy in 1880. Bell himself became very wealthy, nearly a billionaire in today's dollars.

American Bell Telephone Company pushed forward with acquisitions of telephone companies across the United States. A company called Long Lines was established to handle long-distance calls across the scattered group of regional Bell companies. This new company, which was to become the American Telephone and Telegraph Company (AT&T), ended up being the custodian of the telephone patents and the headquarters for research, legal, and financial functions for the whole federation of Bell operating companies. The new company contained a unit called Western Electric, an in-house manufacturer of telephone equipment (formed earlier through the merger of about a half dozen other manufacturers).

⁜

In the early years of the telephone, sets were sold in pairs and were connected directly to each other. The sets were used just for communication from point A to point B. A major advance occurred when, instead of connecting phones directly to each other, they were connected to an exchange in a central office. With all phone lines coming into one central location, an operator could pick up an incoming call and connect it to any one of the other lines coming into the exchange.

The emergence of telephone exchanges also opened the door to some minor inconveniences still with us today. In particular, they were to make solicitation by telephone possible. In 1878, an agent for the Rose-Belford Publishing Company, said to be the first-ever telephone salesperson in Canada, figured that one man would not be able to resist a pitch over the wires. So he rang up Alexander Graham Bell in Brantford and gave him his sales pitch. As the agent went through his spiel, the esteemed inventor listened carefully. When it ended, Bell congratulated the sales agent on his nice manner and said he would take a copy of the book he was selling.

A big issue in the early days was what should be the proper greeting when answering the telephone. The inventor's father advocated "Hoy Hoy," based upon the nautical salutation "Ahoy." The matter was decided however at the first annual convention of the telephone industry in 1880, when the greeting "Hello" was adopted. Father Bell had the last laugh, though. At the conference, label cards were printed up for those in favor of the phrase "'Hello." But a printer's error resulted in the cards reading "O Hell."

The first operators hired to work the switchboards were teenage boys, whose skills as messengers in telegraph offices were thought to be transferable to the new line of work. This proved not to be the case. By most accounts, they were an unruly lot and displayed a propensity for horsing around, eavesdropping on callers, and interrupting at particularly sensitive moments in the conversations.

The boy operators were gradually displaced by female operators, the "Hello Girls" who responded to incoming calls with a bright "Hello." Managers found that they were more alert, courteous, and patient. Dealing with a rude subscriber, they were more likely to retain a professional manner rather than to issue a challenge to come down to the central office and fight it out. In addition, their voices were thought to be more suitable to telecommunication, coming across clearer and more pleasant to the ear.

The first telephone to be put on the market, in 1877, resembled a wooden box camera with one hole in the front for both speaking and listening. Users had to shift the box from ear to mouth to carry out a telephone conversation. Later in the same year, the hole at the front was replaced by a gooseneck-shaped device attached by wire to the box. Subscribers, however, found it was even more convenient to attach a second handle to use for speaking while the other was confined to listening.

In 1876, iron wire was used to transmit telephone calls. A single wire joined two locations, with the wire at both ends connected to the ground so that the earth could provide a return path for the circuit. This system had worked well for telegraphy but turned out to be inadequate for telephony. Voice transmissions were at the mercy of atmospheric conditions and nearby electrical currents. This problem with interference became known as induction.

In the early days, some observers called the telephone device a comparative failure because of this problem. Subscribers complained of meaningless noises on their lines. According to one account, there were noises of sputtering, bubbling, rasping, whistling, and screaming. There was the rustling of leaves, croaking of frogs, hissing of steam, and flapping of bird wings. There were clicks from telegraph wires, cross talk from other telephone lines, and curious little squeals unlike any known sound. Night was nosier than the day, and "at the ghostly hour of midnight, for what strange reasons no one knows, the babel was at its height."[1]

The solution was a lead-covered cable made of seven or more rubber-insulated iron wires strung up on roofs or telephone poles as high as fifty to sixty feet. By 1890, the telephone lines had expanded to the point where the poles and wires darkened the sky in some cities. Complaints from urban dwellers and local governments mounted. But legislation had given the telephone companies the right to erect the grid of poles and wires as long as it did not interfere with the public right of traveling. So the protests met with limited success.

Eventually, the pressure led to a switch to cables laid underground. A method of drawing the cable into an iron pipe filled with oil helped reduce the induction problem. However, it did not remove it completely, and subscribers still complained about problems communicating over cross talk and other noises. In the late 1880s, copper wire started to replace iron wire since it was found to be a better conductor and helped alleviate the problem of fading signals and intermittent background noise. Copper subsequently became the main metal used for telephone wires during the twentieth century (but is now losing ground as fiber-optic materials come on stream).

2

Nortel's Baby Steps

In 1879, Bell's father sold the Canadian patent for the telephone to William Forbes and the American Bell Telephone Company. A steep price was paid, but Forbes saw an opportunity to earn a return several times greater than his principal. Two Canadian telegraph companies—the Dominion Telegraph Company (licensed by Bell's father) and Montreal Telegraph Company (which owned rights to Edison's telephone)—were embroiled in a rivalry so fierce that they were giving away telephone service for free to attract customers. Forbes believed he could bring an end to the bitter contest by getting the two companies to sell their troublesome telephone sidelines to him if he promised to stay out of the telegraph market. Once in possession of the telephone operations, he would merge them and restore profit margins in the Canadian telephone industry.

In 1880, Forbes hired a former ship captain, Charles Fleet-wood Sise, to act as his agent for the planned consolidation in Canada. Sise looked every bit the skipper, possessing a ramrod straight posture and large bushy mustache. One observer noted that a glance from his ice-water blue eyes was sufficient to send recalcitrant employees "looking around for a quarterdeck to swab."[1] Following his seagoing days, he had become an executive in the insurance industry, where he had met Forbes.

After his arrival in Canada in March 1880, Sise obtained a charter from the Canadian parliament to operate a telephone company. This charter, for a company called the Bell Telephone Company of Canada, would be the vehicle for the consolidation of the fragmentary Canadian telephone industry. By the end of 1881, the wheeling and dealing was done, and Bell Telephone Company of Canada could claim ownership over nearly all 3,000 telephones then in use in Canada.

The American Bell Telephone Company retained an influential interest in the new corporation, receiving a large portion of the issued stock in compensation for the transfer of patent rights and the assets acquired from Dominion Telegraph and other companies. Thus was created the forerunner to Bell Canada, the dominant telephone company in Canada to this day (and ultimately the parent company of Nortel Networks for 104 years). The senior executive in control of the Montreal-based company for the first three decades was Sise.

⌗

The first manufacturer of telephone equipment in Canada was James Cowherd. He lived just three miles from the Bell family and was one of the onlookers at the first demonstrations of the telephone near Brantford. Cowherd was a young mechanic and electrician who had experience making steam engines and pipe organs. He accepted an invitation from Bell to go to Boston and learn how to make telephones at the Charles Williams Company, the shop where the first generation of instruments were being fabricated. Upon his return to Canada, Cowherd commenced manufacturing operations in a three-story building located behind his father's hardware store.

Cowherd started out filling the equipment orders flowing in from the marketing efforts of Bell's father and his agents, but when the Canadian patent was sold to American Bell Telephone Company, he became the supplier to its Canadian affiliate, Bell Canada. The option of simply importing the telephones from the Boston shop might have made more economic sense, but that was out of the question. Not only was the duty on imports prohibitive, but Canadian patent law specified that new inventions had to be manufactured in Canada within a year or two of their birth; otherwise their patent would be nullified.

By January 1881, Cowherd had filled nearly 2,500 orders and was starting work on a transmitter and switchboard of his own design. Two months later, just as everything was looking so promising, the thirty-one-year-old Cowherd died of tuberculosis, the same disease that had brought Bell to North America. The *Scientific American* magazine mourned his passing: "If Mr. Cowherd had lived, he would have greatly advanced electrical science."[2]

Cowherd's death left Bell Canada without an equipment supplier. It was a hard blow because equipment could not be imported easily, and existing Canadian suppliers did not have the knowledge or experience to provide product up to standards. For about a year after Cowherd's death, Bell Canada could not obtain quality equipment.

A decision was therefore made to set up a manufacturing and repair department within the Canadian company, and they scouted the factory in Boston looking for a manager. A key individual in that operation, Charles Brown, was hired. He started work on July 24, 1882, with a staff of two persons in a tiny factory on Craig Street in Montreal. By the end of the year, the new Mechanical Department had a staff of thirteen. The hourly wage was less than $1 and the work day was 10 hours long, starting at 7:00 AM. Latecomers would find the doors locked between 7:00 and 8:00 AM, at which time they would be admitted, minus an hour's pay.

The plant on Craig Street was largely an assembly operation putting together components and materials shipped in from Western Electric, the manufacturing arm of American Bell Telephone Company. Over the 1880s, business grew with the rising popularity of telephones. In 1891, the staff of 200 moved to a larger factory erected on Aqueduct Street in Montreal. These new premises were furnished in stages with additional machinery to meet the continuing growth in demand for telephones.

Looking for ways to keep production humming throughout the year, management sought to diversify into other kinds of equipment. But the 1880 parliamentary charter (amended in 1882) for Bell Canada allowed it to manufacture only telephone equipment. To get around this, President Sise spun off the manufacturing division of his company as a separate corporation. On December 7, 1895, Northern Electric and Manufacturing Company was established by Dominion Charter. Bell Canada retained a majority ownership of the newly issued stock in the company. Headquartered in Montreal with Sise in the top position of president, this was the first incarnation of Nortel Networks.

Following the birth of Nortel, the diversification of product lines went ahead. Fire alarms became an important item, to the point where they appeared alongside telephones in the company logo. The production of sleigh bells was significant enough to qualify Nortel as the largest manufacturer in the world at the time. Starting in 1900, a line of phonograph products was added. These and other products were sold on open markets to a variety of customers.

Concerning its core line of telephone equipment, Nortel remained virtually the sole supplier to Bell Canada under a preferential buying arrangement that did not even seek bids or quotations from other possible suppliers. This arrangement evolved over subsequent decades into a less-restrictive format whereby the right of first proposal was bestowed on Nortel in exchange for a commitment to charge prices at least as low as those charged to other companies. In any event, Nortel was solidly placed in its early stages. It had the security of guaranteed sales from Bell Canada, yet also the opportunity for growth in supplying other telephone companies and customers outside of the telephone industry.

In 1914, Bell Canada merged its cable manufacturing subsidiary, Imperial Wire and Cable Company, with Nortel. The new entity was owned 50 percent by Bell Canada, 44 percent by Western Electric Company, and 6 percent by others. At the time of the merger, Nortel consolidated its diverse facilities into a new manufacturing plant on Shearer Street in Montreal. It was not a pleasant place in the beginning. During the first few years of operation, temperatures on the production line during the winter seldom rose above 55 degrees Fahrenheit, compelling workers to wear thick clothing. One old-timer joked that he was a very efficient worker just because he had to keep moving to stay warm. And company folklore has it that amorous employees caught embracing in the hidden nooks and crannies of the plant would claim that they were just trying to keep warm.

The opening of the new facilities proved to be good timing. The expanded production capacity was immediately put to work producing materials for the Allied armies in World War I. The federal government of Canada gave Nortel many contracts for the war effort. Shells, bullet casings, fuses, primers, cartridge clips, signal lamps, and other equipment all rolled out the plant door at a breakneck pace. Shell output, for example, reached 12,000 per week before the war ended. Particularly useful were Nortel's field telephones and switchboards, which enhanced the ability to coordinate military maneuvers on the battlefield.

From its incorporation in 1895 to 1948, Nortel was a family-run business, with Charles Sise and his two sons, Edward and Paul, occupying key executive positions at various times. Charles himself was president until 1913. Then Edward took over from 1913 to 1919, followed by Paul, who was president from 1919 to 1948.

Paul Sise, who held the top job for nearly thirty years, graduated from McGill University in 1901 with a Bachelor of Science degree, and joined Nortel in 1904 as secretary treasurer. He served during World War I as a captain with the London War Office and later with the British Recruiting Mission in the US. Running Nortel after the war, he is said to have had an ability to inspire a spirit of loyalty and service in others. The

1930s were a trying time for Sise, not only because of faltering business and the odious task of laying off people, but also because his one son was killed in a train wreck on Christmas Day, 1934.

A journalist wrote in 1931 that Sise had the characteristic frankness of one who has received a scientific education. He further noted that Sise spoke with almost a military directness, but in kind and even tones. A senior-level employee recalled several decades later that "Sise was one of the old-time gentlemen. You couldn't visualize him ever … being harsh. His brother was in the Bell; his father was the founder. It was a club-like atmosphere as far as he was concerned."[3]

Rather than any particular individual, probably the most important influence on Nortel over its first five decades was the close ties to US telephone interests, which largely consigned Nortel to life as a branch plant. The company's major function was to make telephone equipment for the Canadian market according to designs supplied under service and technical agreements with Western Electric. Instructors, manufacturing experts, and other specialists came on assignment to provide technical assistance. In turn, staff from Nortel would visit Western Electric, where they had wide-open access to information in such vital areas as tools, machines, and test sets. Payment for the technical information and assistance was based on a percentage of sales, so if business was good, Nortel paid more, and if business was poor, Nortel paid less.

One of the main product lines made under Western Electric guidance during the branch plant decades were telephone switches or exchanges, those complex machines that direct calls to their desired destination over the telephone network. In the early years of telephone systems, these switches were manually operated. Nortel's mainstay in the early days was the Standard Magneto Switchboard. It resembled a wide grandfather clock except that the top front half contained a panel full of slots and the middle had a desk full of plugs and wires. Operators would sit in front of the desk and move the plugs into the slots in the panel as calls came in.

Subscribers were aware that operators of manual switchboards were able to listen to whatever conversation was in progress. The potential for eavesdropping and interference became a concern for Kansas City undertaker Almond Strowger. He had become so convinced that the operators on his line were redirecting his business calls to rivals that he set about inventing a device to eliminate them. By the time he discovered the cause of his missing calls—a metal sign outside his building was short-circuiting his incoming messages—he had invented the first automatic telephone exchange.

The Strowger Automatic, which brought the rotary dial telephone into existence, was first patented in 1891 in the United States. But promoters were unable to get it tested because the existing telephone systems would not allow equipment of uncertain quality to be connected to their system. Those restrictions were not in force in remote parts of Canada, so the first installations of the Strowger switch occurred in 1892, when independent telephone companies in locations such as Arnprior, Ontario, and Terrebone, Quebec, experimented with the new device. But the cables and batteries were so crude that the switches functioned only spasmodically. It was not until better batteries and cables were available that the feasibility of the step-by-step exchange was demonstrated in 1905 in Edmonton and Calgary.

With these improvements, the Strowger switch met with more success. In Canada, urban dial service was introduced in

1924 when Bell Canada set up, with the assistance of Nortel and Western Electric, an automated central office at the Grover Exchange in Toronto. For several years after, Nortel was kept busy building and installing automatic exchanges in other Canadian metropolitan areas, until by 1942, 72 percent of Bell telephones in Canada had dial service and were establishing connections without the assistance of an operator on most local calls.

The next generation of automated switches to come was the "cross-bar" variety. These switches essentially consisted of a set of horizontal and vertical bars that could be moved by electromagnets to make contacts at selected intersections. Stimulated by the pattern of electrical impulses from the dialed call, the electromagnets would relay a call by establishing any suitable arrangement of connections at intersections throughout the matrix. The advantages were greater speed, reliability, smaller size, and lower cost. New services, such as push-button key pads and direct intercity dialing also became possible.

Although Nortel was closely tied to Western Electric, it was still able to manufacture and/or distribute many nontelephone products on its own. Early efforts, as mentioned, included fire alarms and phonographs, but by the 1920s, Nortel was also a distributor of a broad array of electrical consumer appliances, including kettles, toasters, cigar lighters, electric stoves, and washing machines—all leading-edge products of their day. For many of these newfangled products, the company was the pioneering and dominant supplier in Canada. Over twenty distribution centers spread across the country were engaged in promotion and marketing activities.

Another independent line of products started in 1922 when Nortel began manufacturing vacuum tubes. Tube No. 208A—the first in Canada—was put to work powering the repeater devices used to boost signals over long distances of the telephone network. Seeking to parlay its vacuum-tube exper-tise to other fields, Nortel expanded into manufacturing radios, and to promote sales, the company set up its own radio station in Montreal and broadcast a mixture of Sunday church services and musical events during the 1920s. Later, in the 1940s, the Northern Electric Hour was a popular radio program.

Another first in Canada was the moving-picture sound sys-tems produced under license. This equipment added sound to silent films at the Palace Theatre in Montreal in 1928. A sub-sidiary established in 1934, Dominion Sound Equipment Ltd., subsequently provided sound services that were used in sev-eral film productions. Acoustic services, such as public address systems, were also part of the lineup. In the late 1930s, the sub-sidiary set up production of marine and aircraft radios in antic-ipation of war and, when war did arrive, the radios went into service in Lancaster bombers and British tanks.

Further diversification of product lines occurred after the war. A big commercial success for Nortel in the late 1940s and early 1950s was the five-tube Baby Champ tabletop radio. Available in six colors, the sets were shown in advertisements with teenagers Nancy and Elizabeth wearing sweaters display-ing the company's initials, N and E. Less successful product lines were the Northern-Hammond organs and tabletop tele-vision sets (with an RCA picture tube).

In 1957, Nortel pulled back from product diversification, selling off its household appliance, radio, and television busi-nesses to focus on the telephone equipment business. Initially, the sidelines made sense because the major distributors of appliances in the early days were power utilities. Since Nortel was already selling cable and related equipment to them, it was profitable to leverage this relationship and also sell appliances to them. But over the years, the utilities handed the distribution of appliances over to electrical retailers, and Nortel had to spend much larger sums on promotion and advertising. This led to losses that dragged down profits earned on telephone equipment production. In short, the appliance and peripheral businesses were no longer profitable, so they were dropped.

#

From its birth in 1895 to the onset of World War II, Nortel grew largely in tandem with the roll-out of telephone systems in Canada, supplying equipment to the dominant Bell Canada in central Canada and to other telephone companies located in other regions. One measure of the expansion of telephone service is reflected in statistics on the number of telephones in Canada: in 1895, there were approximately 28,000 telephone sets, but by 1942 the number had risen to 925,000—an increase of over 3,200 percent.

Nortel's upward path over the first half of the century, however, was not a smooth one. Although it enjoyed considerable security as a preferred supplier to Bell Canada, general economic conditions caused fluctuations in fortunes. The 1920s were a particularly good time because of the economic boom, and in 1929, the company had 7,000 employees compared to 2,500 in 1922. But the 1930s were a big bust, and by 1933 the employee population had shrunk back to 2,500. Things improved a bit by 1939, but the number of employees still numbered only 3,700.

During the depression of the 1930s, financial losses mounted, reaching $750,000 (Canadian) in 1933. Telephone subscribers were canceling their telephone leases en masse (the volume of returned sets exceeded 100,000 in 1934), pushing Nortel to the edge of the precipice. What saved the company

was a loan of nearly $1 million from Western Electric and ongo-
ing business from Bell Canada. So, having close corporate connections and being a branch plant did have its benefits.

When World War II broke out, the Canadian government
put a freeze on all production not related to military purposes.
That included telephones. But Nortel prospered—orders for
war material boosted company sales by 2.5 times in 1941 over
1939. Running around the clock during the war, the company
supplied more than a million artillery fuses, those triggers
located in the tip of shells to set them off. In addition to supplying wireless sets for two-way communication in tanks and
other vehicles, Nortel contributed to the war effort by producing the top-secret magnetron tubes used in radar equipment,
one of the most valuable weapons the Allied forces had.

The end of the war meant a sudden falloff in government
contracts, but at the same time there was a huge demand for
consumer products. Large backlogs for products were on the
books—in the case of telephones, there were unfilled orders
for 77,000 units shortly after peace was restored. Over the next
five years, more than a million telephone sets were installed,
which was, of course, a huge boom for Nortel. Including other
commercial successes such as the Baby Champ radio, the bottom line for Nortel was quite healthy throughout the 1940s
and 1950s.

⚜

The patent and commercial agreements signed with Western
Electric gave Nortel the exclusive right to build products according to the designs of the leading manufacturer of telecommunication equipment. The technical information agreements
entitled Nortel to receive technical assistance relating to the conversion of basic product designs to manufacturing processes.

Access to Western Electric personnel also facilitated the modification of engineering drawings for the purpose of adapting the designs to the specific needs of the Canadian market.

In exchange for licensing its designs, Western Electric received a royalty on sales in Canada. Thus, the agreements were a way for Western Electric to enter the Canadian market for telecommunication equipment, and for its part, Nortel was able to offer telecommunication equipment without much fear of competition. If a potential rival appeared, they would face litigation on the grounds of patent violation. If that was not enough of a deterrent, then there were the mighty resources of Western Electric standing behind Nortel. These very effective barriers protected Nortel in the Canadian market.

The turning point in the relationship with Western Electric began when the US Department of Justice filed a suit in 1949 alleging that Western Electric was monopolizing the manufacture and supply of communication equipment and was therefore in violation of the *Sherman Antitrust Act*. At the time, Western Electric supplied equipment to 82 percent of the telephone carrier industry, the portion controlled by its parent, AT&T. Government lawyers sought to remedy the situation by compelling AT&T to divest itself of Western Electric.

The legal proceedings went on for several years. Finally, in 1956, an out-of-court settlement, a "consent decree," was reached under which AT&T and Western Electric were allowed to remain together in exchange for making patent holdings available without charge and releasing technical information to outside suppliers. AT&T and Western Electric were also constrained from competing for business among the 18 percent of the telephone carrier industry still independent of AT&T.

This consent decree was a main factor leading to the withdrawal of Western Electric from the Canadian market. The patent and information agreements with Nortel became more restrictive and expensive, and they were finally terminated in the middle of the 1960s. The agreements were ended because Western Electric was afraid their liberal provisions would have to be extended to other companies in North America under the terms of the deal signed with the US Justice Department.

Western Electric was also worried, some observers say, that Nortel might use the expertise in the agreements to launch an export drive targeting independent US telephone carriers. Such a development might be interpreted by the Justice Department as a covert move to market to the US independents using Nortel as a stalking-horse.

Recognizing that there was no longer any commercial reason to be in Canada, AT&T and Western Electric sold off their interests in Bell Canada and Nortel in stages. The divestiture of the latter was completed in 1962, with Bell Canada taking over the Western Electric interest; AT&T's interest in Bell Canada was reduced to 2 percent during the 1960s and then disappeared in the middle of the 1970s.

3

A Triumvirate Wakes a Sleepy Company

Nortel's metamorphosis into a dynamic and innovative enterprise did not happen overnight. In fact, for the better part of the 1960s, the transition was a struggle. When the break came from Western Electric in the late 1950s, staff shouted hooray for independence, but afterward the company's performance was lackluster. As a result, Bell Canada had its subsidiary under continuous review over the 1950s and 1960s and, at various times, it seriously considered selling Nortel.

Senior executives at Nortel report that the greatest problem over the decade was changing the ingrained culture that had built up over the sixty-five years the company had been a preferred supplier to Bell Canada. The company had earned its keep largely by adapting and manufacturing Western Electric products for Bell Canada. Marketing and design were virtually nonexistent in Nortel. The overall atmosphere was, according to one observer, "sleepy"; another added that it was the kind of company where one could get fired only "for screwing the boss's daughter, and then only if it was on company premises."[1]

The turning point came under the leadership of a triumvirate. Robert Scrivener, president of Bell Canada, was the cunning strategist with the vision. Walter Light, executive vice president of operations of Bell Canada, was the loyal lieutenant who was the heart and soul of the team. John Lobb, chief executive of Nortel during the early seventies, was the tough-as-nails lieutenant who bulldozed his way into the company.

Scrivener, the son of a Bell Canada lineman, joined the company at the end of the Great Depression as a switchboard operator. Although he was not trained as an engineer (his undergraduate degree was in history), he acquired a detailed knowledge of Bell Canada's operations by working in almost every division during the 1940s and 1950s. In 1961, he was promoted to vice president of finance, and in 1968, he became president.

Trim and erect in bearing, the six-foot Scrivener radiated candor and sincerity. As befit his humble origins, he was a man with a common touch; he was at home chatting with employees at every rank, from repairmen to senior executives. His easygoing manner made him many friends outside the company, including the members of parliament with whom he discussed regulatory matters. Many executives at AT&T and its subsidiaries were also good friends as a result of attending conferences of the Bell companies while Bell Canada was still part of the family.

Behind "the ever-present cloud of cigarette smoke and the horn-rimmed glasses were eyes that saw big dreams."[2] As president of Bell Canada, Scrivener was responsible for setting the strategic direction of Bell Canada and Nortel. The part of his job he relished the most was envisioning what telephone systems would be like within the next five to ten years and then deciding what would have to be done to get there. It was a task he truly savored, for he viewed business as a creative pursuit wherein satisfaction was derived from setting and realizing goals.

Assisting him in the formation of a strategy for Nortel was his second-in-command, Walter Light. A "lanky, gawky sort of fellow who talks like a down-home, cornpone Jimmy Stewart character,"[3] according to one description. Light was born in the remote mining town of Cobalt in northern Ontario. He might have ended up working underground in the mines like so many others he grew up with, but he had bigger dreams. He got a degree in science from one of Canada's top schools, Queen's University, and then joined Bell Canada, where he rose through the ranks. Despite his success at climbing the corporate ladder, Light was known for being unpretentious and a straight shooter who spoke his mind. He had a spirit of unbridled enthusiasm that inspired those around him.

In the late 1960s, a committee of Bell Canada executives was again deciding whether Nortel had a future. A lot of cash had been plowed into the subsidiary, yet it was not paying off. As a member of the review committee, Light did a study outlining a strategy that was instrumental in determining Nortel's direction over the next two decades. Key recommendations in the report were that the company should become the low-cost producer in the industry, a leader in technology, and infused with a more aggressive and dynamic culture.

Endorsing the vision outlined in the report, Scrivener agreed to exploratory studies into the development of digital telephone switches. Thus, Scrivener was "the architect of change," as one career executive at Bell Canada called him. Light echoed this view: "The whole push from analog to digital was managed by Scrivener. It was Bob who really saw that we had to go down the digital path."[4] In doing so, Scrivener had perceived the implications of the new electronic technologies ahead of senior management at AT&T; his vision was the spark plug that got Nortel out front of the US telecommunication behemoth.

It was a radical departure. The required scale of research and development would be bigger than the Canadian market could support, so Nortel would need to make a commitment to expand its sales via exports into the United States. It was a risky course of action in that Nortel would not have any guarantee of making sufficient sales; there were no preferred supplier relationships in this arena, just a competitive bidding process in the segment of the US telephone industry still unaffiliated with AT&T.

To position Nortel as one of the lowest-cost manufacturers for the planned attack of the US market, a major shake-up was initiated with the hiring in May 1971 of fifty-eight-year-old John Lobb as chief executive. Observers described him as compact and sturdy, with the broad chin of Winston Churchill and the steady gaze of John Wayne. His mouth curled down even when he smiled. A man of contrasts, he had a considerate side but also was a tough guy; he had a sense of humor but also was a no-nonsense person who commanded attention.

He started out as a lawyer in Minnesota, and then he went on to work at ITT Corp. where he became known as an aggressive Mr. Fix-It. He seemed for a time to be the heir to the chief executive position but was passed over. He quit to head up the failing Crucible Steel Company of Pittsburgh, and after two years of radical restructuring, he made it one of the most profitable companies in the steel industry.

Lobb's arrival signaled the start of a radical transformation at Nortel. Denzil Doyle, a former president of Digital Equipment of Canada (which had dealings with Nortel in the 1970s), saw:

> ... an incredible transformation take place under John Lobb... he brought all the same management principles— management by objective and all of those good things [from ITT]... today those principles are still there and Nortel has somehow managed to keep that culture.[5]

Gordon Hutchinson, a founder of the Canadian Advanced Technology Association, was another observer during the Lobb era. He would agree with Doyle's assessment.

> John Lobb came in and he eviscerated the place... What he did was get rid of the deadwood... he stripped down and cleaned up and gave something [for future managers] to build on.[6]

During his first year, Lobb traveled over 100,000 miles visiting company plants and offices across Canada. He wanted to make his presence felt and to take stock of the situation. What he found was not appealing. He recalled: "There were design engineering problems, there were production problems, very bad marketing problems, and financial controls were weak."[7] In his opinion, Nortel was in desperate need of new blood: "Because of the nature of the business and the way it was directed, there hadn't been enough strong men attracted to Northern [Nortel] in the last twenty years."[8]

In response, Lobb set up a monthly reporting system whereby managers had to update him on their performance, a form of management by objective. He issued a directive that operations were to focus on only profitable product lines and discard the losers or outsource them to other suppliers who could turn them out more efficiently. All divisions were ordered to find efficiencies and to slash costs, including payrolls. Headquarters was a particular target for cuts—only a few senior executives escaped the wide swath of the ax.

Lobb believed that attitudes at the company could be fundamentally changed only with a clean sweep of the broom from top to bottom. He "fired people... on the spot."[9] General management meetings were one forum for discharging staff. A Bell Canada official recalled that one day Lobb turned to an executive who was giving a presentation and said: "You take those charts, and you roll them up and shove them right up your ass, and go collect your paycheck."[10]

Stiff medicine of this kind had its dangers for the administering doctor. The recipients often did not go quietly and sometimes complained to higher-ups. Lobb, however, had the full backing of Scrivener and powerful allies in the Bell Canada boardroom. Scrivener did occasionally get upset with Lobb's rough-and-ready approach, but the two remained on good terms. Their friendship was replenished on the golf links; both were members of an exclusive golf club in Pennsylvania, where they would play a round or two together on weekends a few times a year.

The change in attitude that Lobb wanted to bring about was that Nortel was in business to make money, not just products. As Roy Merrills, an executive during the Lobb years, says:

> That was a big change. If you've been the captive supplier
> to Bell Canada, you're not really concerned about making
> money, you're concerned about making product. What
> John Lobb did was to come in from ITT and bring in their

highly disciplined, business plan-based culture. He would come up to an employee and ask: "What do we make?" And God help you if you said switching. He'd say, "We don't make switching, goddamn it. We make money."... He changed everything.[11]

To spearhead the drive into the US market, Lobb set up a US subsidiary, (then called Northern Telecom Inc.), in 1971. Setting up shop in AT&T's backyard risked incurring the formidable wrath of the giant, so Scrivener flew down to reassure John De Butts, chairman and chief executive officer of AT&T, that Nortel would go after only the business communication market and the independent phone companies. Scrivener's friendship with De Butts—the two men used to share a drink or two after conferences of the Bell group of companies in the 1950s and 1960s—helped them reach an agreement.

In 1973, Nortel filed an initial public offering of shares on the Toronto Stock Exchange. Two years later, its shares were also listed for trading on the New York Stock Exchange, not just to raise money but also to raise the profile of Nortel in the US market. Lobb was no stranger to stock markets. While at ITT, he had been instrumental in the conglomerate's initial public offering and carried out nearly thirty acquisitions of other companies.

At Nortel, he was involved in acquisitions as part of the company's attempt to build up its product portfolio. One of these got him into a bit of hot water. In the fall of 1974, Nortel made a bid for control for Dictaphone Corp., a maker of dictating and answering machines. Management at Dictaphone responded with a vociferous counterattack, initiating lawsuits charging Nortel with violation of antitrust and fraud laws. It was a very hostile takeover attempt.

A day before the offer was to expire, Nortel canceled its bid, and Dictaphone's share price plunged by nearly 40 percent. This surprise withdrawal left Neuberger and Berman, an arbitrage firm on Wall Street, with a $100,000 loss, prompting a civil lawsuit seeking to recoup that money as well as $3 million for injured private investors. In their suit, the brokerage firm claimed that fraud provisions of security laws had been violated because John Lobb's wife, allegedly acting on inside information, had secretly bought shares in Dictaphone weeks before the unsuccessful bid for control.

The amount of shares bought by Mrs. Lobb mentioned in the civil action was rather insignificant—only 1,000 at a price just under $8. For her part, when interviewed by the media, she resolutely maintained that she had no prior knowledge of the takeover bid, frequently invested on her own, and that it was all a matter of coincidence. Nortel and Lobb denied all the charges and filed a legal defense in a US federal court. Both were subsequently exonerated.

Despite this spot of temporary trouble, Lobb's track record at Nortel was impressive, at least in terms of the bottom line. In the first year of his duties, profits (in Canadian dollars) soared from $5 million to $13 million, and in the next year, they nearly doubled to $25 million. His impact on corporate culture was a major legacy too. By the end of his term, Nortel was a brand-new company. The inward-looking firm that had been focused on manufacturing had been turned into an outward-looking and aggressive company focused on making a profit. Walter Benger, an executive who worked with Lobb declared: "Our big break was getting Lobb because he broke down the inertia within Northern and was keen to go after the US market. He said, enough of the studies, here's what we're going to do."[12]

By 1976, the triumvirate was still in control but were in new positions. In that year, Lobb left the chief executive position at headquarters for the top job at Nortel's US subsidiary, and Scrivener left Bell Canada to become chairman and CEO of Nortel. Light, had left the Bell Canada executive in 1974 to become president of Nortel (and became CEO in 1979 when Scrivener retired). To leave Bell Canada for Nortel might be seen as a step down for Scrivener and Light, but that is where the two men wanted to go because the action was more interesting to them.

As president, Light played an instrumental role in guiding Nortel over the second half of the 1970s and early 1980s. He believed that getting anything done in a meaningful way required challenging people until they were very nearly at the point of rebellion. As he said:

> I worked people at their maximum stress level so they felt free to bitch. I didn't want to take a contented army to war. What you need is creative tension, and we had plenty of that. People would come to me and complain, "Jeez, I'm working too hard'" and I would say, "OK, I'll take away some of your responsibilities." Of course, the moment I threatened to reduce their authority, they would start flapping their wings and moan, "Oh no! I didn't mean it. No way." Then they'd work twice as hard.[13]

Light practiced tough love before the term was coined. His approach created a demanding workplace environment, one aimed at winning commitment to the organization. A tireless worker himself, Light made sure he set the proper example. Employees who were not prepared to give their all to the company usually did not last long or were quickly surpassed on the corporate ladder.

His management style was not one of issuing directives but of finding the best people for the job and challenging them with tough questions. It was a technique for getting subordinates to think for themselves. Workers acting on something they have thought of themselves are likely to be more motivated than those acting on an order. To this end, Light held executive meetings at which key operating staff, including the young engineers running divisions, would be required to explain what they were doing, why they were doing it, and what they were planning to do next. He let them take the initiative, but he used a questioning process to stay in touch and guide wayward initiatives back to the fold.

Lacking any clear direction, many employees found the environment stressful. Some could not take it and left, but those who were willing to think for themselves flourished. Still, many employees felt off balance, a state Light reputedly liked to create. One trick was his habit of reading mail while listening to an executive give a presentation at a meeting. Another was his practice of writing WOW or CAIC on memos sent to his office. Asked one day by an executive about the meaning of the notations, he replied:

> If you get a WOW, that could mean one of two things. That you should be proud of what you've done or that you're in real trouble. As for the CAIC, it just means "Christ, Am I Confused." Any questions?[14]

At his farewell speech at the 1985 Annual Meeting, he expanded upon his management philosophy this way:

> The most successful corporate leaders are content to provide the conceptualization of their corporation's roles and provide the direction and thrust of future endeavors. Beyond that, they hire the finest talent available at any given

point in time, bring them on board, give them their trust, challenge them, comfort them when they stumble, and provide them with the widest opportunity to grow, innovate, succeed, and challenge those below them.[15]

Under Light, the corporate culture became one of challenging each other. If somebody said something that was not clear, others would challenge the speaker. Better to clear up the matter than go away under a cloud of uncertainty. As such, the Nortel culture was distinct from the typical US corporate culture of team play. In the mid-1980s, Tom Peters, a top US management consultant, was called in to look at Nortel practices, and ended up asking (in effect): "Why do you guys hate each other?" To him, it was easy to see this kind of environment as adversarial rather than one of challenging one another. Light's successor, Edmund Fitzgerald, used the term "warring tribes" to describe what he saw. Upon retirement, Fitzgerald was given a referee shirt and a golden whistle because he said his role as chief executive at Nortel was more like being an arbitrator.

As such, Light was a contributor, along with Scrivener and Lobb, to waking up Nortel from its half century of slumberlike existence as a company that simply reproduced the licensed designs of one company for another. The three men were good friends, had great respect for one another, and worked well together. Together, the three created a dynamic and demanding culture that started with a vision of where the company had to go in order to bring about the next stage in the evolution of telecommunication systems. Then it challenged employees to find ways of achieving goals within the given constraints of time and cost. It led to a results-orientated type of environment, full of competition within the ranks.

A sense of the work culture left behind by the 1970s revolution is provided in an employment guidebook published in the mid-1980s. One Nortel employee is quoted as saying:

> Most people here love the stress. They want to be stretched, to know where their limits are. And you do have to sacrifice things—like taking the kids to the hockey game. If the work pressure is there, by Christ you stay at work until the job is done... Those unwilling to let work cut into home life need not apply for jobs here. Within [Nortel], unless you are willing to make those sacrifices, you might end up not having a job.[16]

Slackers, indeed, need not apply. It is rumored that one way Nortel used to weed out the lazy at the recruitment stage was to schedule job interviews at 9:00 AM on Sunday morning. Those who asked for another time were granted it but they may have lost a few points in their overall assessment.

That the workforce at Nortel was willing to adapt to the demanding pace and continuous state of flux is perhaps a reflection of the predominance of youth in the ranks, particularly in the research divisions where the average age is under 30. Most people this young are still out to prove themselves in the workplace, to establish that they can do the job. So they are prepared to work hard and accept challenges. Many have yet to start a family, so they have more time and energy to focus on the company. They are also a source of fresh ideas and innovation— important assets for finding solutions to the many problems that pop up in a rapidly changing industry.

In return for all their hard work, Nortel employees receive one of the best remuneration packages anywhere in their job categories. Aside from attractive salaries, there is a very generous benefits program containing excellent medical, dental, and pension plans, along with supplementary maternity benefits. The company is willing to pay tuition for university courses, and it provides work-site facilities such as fitness rooms to help employees thrive. With the stellar performance of Nortel's stock in the late 1990s, the shareownership plan has left many employees well off and happy to be part of the team.

4

New
Beginnings
and
False Starts

The winding down of the commercial and technical service agreements with AT&T and Western Electric presented Bell Canada with a challenge. Where would it get new designs for upgrading equipment and components in its telephone system? Should it look for other companies from which to license designs, or should it set up a research and development division at Nortel so that its preferred supplier could do its own product development?

The decision was to go for in-house research and development, launching what was to become a main source of disruptive technologies for the next four decades in the telecommunication industry. It was the origin of the line of digital telephone switches that revolutionized telephone networks throughout the 1970s and into the 1990s, effectively turning them into vast computer networks. It was also the origin of many advances in wireless communication and the fiber-optic systems that carry the majority of traffic on the Internet in the early 2000s. The sales and earnings brought about by these new products are what boosted Nortel into the big leagues of the networking industry in the 2000s.

A preliminary question concerned where the research department should go. The location ultimately chosen, in 1959, was just outside Ottawa, the capital of Canada. The main attraction was the proximity to the scientific community employed at the Defence Research Board and the National Research Council. These two governmental agencies had scientists working in areas in which Nortel was interested, so closeness would aid in the exchange of ideas. The Defence Research Board furthermore offered training courses in advanced technologies such as transistors, and it was authorized to pass on its technological discoveries to the private sector. Two academic institutions, the University of Ottawa and Carleton University, rounded out the knowledge base, offering technical courses for employees interested in upgrading their skills.

Responsibility for pulling a research team together fell to Brewer Hunt, vice president of research and development. Hunt was known to have a stern business hand, but he also knew how to have fun and lighten up the atmosphere. On Fridays, he would stand up from his desk and balance a glass on his head to signal that it was time to head out for a drink. On Mondays, however, it was all back to business.

One of Hunt's main tasks was the recruitment of skilled engineers and scientists. To carry this out, he set up a program to visit universities across Canada and meet with professors who could identify promising talent. Much like a hockey scout visiting farm teams, candidates in science and engineering graduate schools would be earmarked and watched. The best and the brightest would be approached with lucrative employment offers.

The recruitment campaign extended outside Canada, and Nortel's willingness to pay top dollar lured many engineers away, in particular, from Britain—a country still recovering from the ravages of World War II and trying to hold back inflation with pay freezes. Hundreds made the trip across the Atlantic, attracted by salaries that were as much as three times higher than they could get at home. One engineering graduate at first thought the amount offered by Nortel was a currency conversion mistake because it was so much higher than the others he had on the table from domestic companies.

This British invasion preceded the more famous one led by the Beatles and had a lasting impact on the course of the technology industry in North America. Many of the British émigrés stayed within Nortel and moved up the ranks to senior positions. Others left to start high-flying technology companies—such as MOSAID Technologies Inc., Newbridge Networks Inc., and Corel Corp.—helping to create in the Ottawa region Silicon Valley North, Canada's largest geographical cluster of technology firms.

The research division's first major project was an assignment from Bell Canada: the design of the SA-1, a small telephone switch that directed calls over the telephone network in rural areas. The assignment was no gift. The design group set up within Nortel had to prepare a bid in competition against an outside provider. The in-house switching group won the contract and proved to be up to the task: they had the SA-1 ready for market by 1961. More than 1,000 SA-1 systems were subsequently sold in Canada and the United States. This early success was a step toward convincing Bell Canada that Nortel's design department was a viable alternative to licensing designs from other manufacturers.

A top priority of the steadily growing research team during the 1960s was to generate as many patents as possible in the field of telecommunication. This was a way to put up a wall of protection against rivals that might attempt to encroach upon the young company's intellectual capital. A recruit fresh out of a British university in 1964, Michael Cowpland, recalls that a bonus of $500 was offered for each patent a research engineer secured.

Cowpland thought it was a great system; it kept him busy over his first four years in the labs, trying to invent as many new things as he could. In the process, he became one of the more productive researchers, obtaining one of the highest number of patents during the 1960s. Eventually the lure of $500 rewards proved insufficient for Cowpland, who would leave Nortel in the early 1970s to ply his innovative talents in search of bigger returns as one of the founders of Mitel Corp, and later as chief executive of Corel Corp.

Throughout the 1960s, research staff at Nortel joined up with staff from the Defence Research Board and National Research Council to look into the potential of semiconductors and integrated circuits for military, space, and private sector uses. By 1966, Nortel's lab within a lab, the Advanced Devices Centre, founded in the late 1950s, had 550 employees working on manufacturing 260 different types of semiconductors. Many of these microchips would perform vital functions in the computerized telephone switches that pushed Nortel past its competition in the 1970s and 1980s.

✣

In January 1971, Bell Canada and Nortel created Bell Northern Research (BNR), a subsidiary in which large parts of Nortel's research and development function would be consolidated. The subsidiary was jointly owned by Bell Canada and Nortel in proportion to their financial contributions—which were 30 and 70 percent, respectively, throughout the 1970s. One reason for the creation of BNR was that it provided a forum for the two companies to coordinate their mutual and increasing involvement as client and producer in the development of the SP-1 and subsequent switches. This close association in which Nortel had full access to the needs, costs, and system characteristics of a telephone carrier was a superb form of market research that gave the equipment manufacturer an important edge.

At first, the financing for BNR came from a central headquarters budget, but soon it came directly from the respective divisions of Nortel that would be manufacturing and selling the new products. As a result, the primary focus of BNR would be more on applications than pure, basic research. This was a central factor behind BNR's and Nortel's successful track record of introducing new products in a more timely manner than its larger rivals over the 1970s and 1980s.

Getting Donald Chisholm to preside over BNR for its first five years was a coup. He was hired by Bell Canada's Scrivener, an avid golfer who played a few rounds a year with several of the top executives in the AT&T family of telephone companies. In search of a president for BNR, he visited one of his golfing buddies, the president of Bell Labs. The latter scribbled two names on a piece of paper and told Scrivener to take his pick—adding that either of the two scientists could succeed him as president of the Bell Labs. One was Chisholm, a graduate of the University of Toronto, and the other was William Baker—a leading chemist who went on to become head of Bell Labs a few years later.

Thus, Scrivener got one of the best scientists from AT&T's Bell Labs to come over to lead BNR. Scrivener's being on good terms with top officials in the AT&T family certainly helped him pull it off, but it appears there was also an element of good luck in that Bell Labs at the time had two equally good contenders for the top job, and did not mind letting one go to an organization they then believed was relatively harmless.

Chisholm is credited with creating the culture that guided BNR until it was split up in the reorganization of the mid-1990s. He strove to bring about the casual and informal style of a university campus, the kind of setting he believed would promote creative thought and the exchange of ideas. Prior to his arrival, staff in the research department wore ties to the office and donned jackets to go to lunch. But Chisholm liked to walk about in the hallways in loafers and an open-collar shirt to chat with employees at all levels. Following his example, dress throughout the organization became casual.

He believed in, to use his own words, "intelligent subversives"—people who liked to stick their necks out, to stir things up, and get new things going. Organizational structures have an inertia that discourages change, and such individuals often get crushed by those who just want to get on with the job as it has always been done before. But in a research organization set up to foster innovation, the intelligent subversives—a select group of 2 to 3 percent of the workforce—have to be encouraged. They need to be watched by management and prodded if they get too far out of line; they need a guardian angel in upper management to protect them from less-farsighted individuals. Chisholm's mission, in short, was to create a unique working environment in which the doers, who need a stable framework, can coexist with the creative individuals trying to upset the apple cart.

Those that knew Chisholm had a great deal of respect for his talents and leadership skills. He could be a bit off the wall as he strolled about the hallways in sock feet and no shoes, quoting Machiavelli and Chairman Mao. A former coworker recalls Chisholm coming into work wearing brown suede shoes, blue shirt, and trousers with the cleaning tag still affixed. Another coworker reports that Chisholm overflowed with ideas, but "he'd be the first to admit that most of them were crazy."[1] However, whenever someone told him something would not work, he would say: "I'll ask you again next week," creating the feeling within the organization that there was little that could not be done.

One risk in presenting the story of a successful company is creating the impression that the rise was a straight line upward. The progress of companies is usually more in the nature of two steps forward and one step backwards. To illustrate the dead ends and detours that can occur along the way, consider Nortel's adventure with Microsystems Inc. in the 1970s.

Microsystems was formed in 1969 when part of Nortel's semiconductor lab was spun off into a separate subsidiary, of which a portion was sold the next year to the public through an initial offering of shares on the Toronto Stock Exchange at $10 each. The impetus for the spin-off came from the Department of Industry in the Canadian federal government. Seeking to develop a domestic microelectronics industry that could reduce Canada's ever-widening trade deficit in electronic products, the department gave Nortel a $30 million (Canadian) grant (to be repaid out of profits), a five-year $12-million (Canadian) interest-free loan, and loan guarantees. In return, Nortel would provide a building just outside Ottawa and invest $24.5 million (Canadian) over five years. Part of the output of microelectronic devices would go into Nortel's own products, while the other part would go toward domestic needs and exports.

In the late 1960s, while Microsystems was being put together, the outlook for semiconductor chip sales was bright. In fact, in 1968, the year the decision was taken to launch, the forecast of 30 percent annual growth had been exceeded. But the semiconductor industry is notoriously cyclical, alternating every three to four years between boom and bust. By the time Microsystems had geared up for production in 1970, the down phase was in progress. Prices were in a precipitous slide, and profits were dissolving into losses everywhere in the industry.

With the down phase dragging on through 1970, losses over the first two years of Microsystems' existence amounted to $13.8 million (Canadian), nearly the same amount as its sales. Besides poor prices and high start-up costs, another factor contributing to the losses was a special charge of $1.6 million (Canadian) to cover the cash that had been invested in the commercial paper of bankrupt Penn Central Transportation Company. Under the weight of its early misfortunes, Microsystems' share price had tumbled 50 percent to $5 by April 1971.

Despite these initial woes, Microsystems came across a chance in 1970 to emerge as the Intel of Canada, indeed, to usurp Intel itself in the field of memory and microprocessor chips. By 1970, Intel had developed a semiconductor memory chip that was cheaper and more powerful than any of the alternatives then starting to emerge. The Intel memory cell used the metal oxide on silicon technique, three instead of four transistors, and fewer interconnections. In allowing cells to be packed more densely, this dynamic random-access memory (DRAM) would store 1,024 bits—four times as much as other types of semiconductor chips.

In response to customers wanting a second supplier, the board of directors at Intel agreed to give Microsystems "second-source" rights to produce their new DRAM memory chip. In exchange for $1 million up front and follow-on royalties, Intel agreed to help Microsystems set up a manufacturing process to make its new memory chip. Afterward, both companies would compete with each other for business.

The history of second sourcing is littered with the debris of young companies that come up with a good idea but fail to mass-produce well enough against the second source to which they have handed over their secrets. And Microsystems, backed by the resources of Nortel and the government of Canada, was well positioned to become a dominant supplier in a market on the cusp of exponential growth.

After securing the right to produce the Intel memory chip, Nortel was visited by Intel personnel who came to deliver the die sets and to get fabrication lines running properly. Three months later, Microsystems had its own version of the DRAM chip rolling out of its plant outside Ottawa. It was now in direct competition with Intel. In the early going, it had the still-fledgling company on the ropes; Intel was losing sales to the point where its executives were complaining in the US media about the subsidies its second source was receiving.

Microsystems then "got too clever."[2] To get more chips out of each wafer, it made a change to its production systems without consulting Intel. The change was a disaster, and production ground to a halt just when demand was recovering for microchips. Worse, its existing customers, strapped for memory circuits, flocked to Intel with large orders for delivery as soon as possible. Intel sales and profitability shot upwards, and its reputation as a company that delivers on time was reinforced.

The technical problems on the production line led to a change of management. Senior executives (led by a chemist,

Olaf Wolff, an executive from the mining industry), were replaced by a team from Nortel. They fixed up the problems and restored production. The new products included the first operational 4K RAM chip and an early microprocessor design. Unfortunately, the rain cloud let forth another shower: just as Microsystems was ready to pump out its chips again, another severe downturn struck the semiconductor industry. The intense competition and price erosion doomed the company to yet another year of losses.

By 1974, the cumulative losses over the past four years amounted to $45 million (Canadian) on sales of $90 million (Canadian), nearly a third of which were to Nortel for telecommunication applications. As the 1974 slump settled in, a decision was taken by Nortel executives and senior civil servants in the Department of Industry to close down their joint venture in order to avoid suffering further losses. Certain assets of the defunct company were taken over by Nortel.

In failing to grasp the opportunity, Nortel missed a chance to become what Intel later became. Instead, Microsystems became a footnote in the annals of the semiconductor industry, known as the company that saved Intel and made it what is today. It was the company whose million-dollar cash payment enabled Intel to ride out the industry downturn of 1970. And later on, as Microsystems gave up on getting DRAM chips to market, it allowed Intel—the sole remaining supplier—to exercise monopolistic influence over a rapidly growing field. As such, Microsystems was the "ideal second source... a company that was just good enough to make customers believe it could build the part, but not quite good enough to actually build it. That was the kind of second source that Intel was lucky enough to find."[3]

Postmortems mention the bad luck in encountering inhospitable market conditions. But they also include stories of mismanagement in the days before Nortel assumed direct control. Two former employees, Michael Cowpland (later involved in building Mitel and Corel) and Terry Mathews (later involved in building Mitel and Newbridge Networks), complained about bureaucratic slowness and a lack of aggressiveness in pursuit of business opportunities. Dick Foss, a former Microsystems chip designer who went on to become chief executive of MOSAID Technologies Inc., refers to a lack of spending controls as a problem. By way of illustration, he cites his own experience— Microsystems was paying to maintain three houses for him, including a fully furnished dwelling in Brussels where he was initially hired.

Despite the losses incurred by the government and Nortel, there is a case to be made that the Microsystems episode actually may have had a net benefit for Canada. It brought together a group of skilled microelectronics personnel that later were to form companies of their own or contribute their expertise to existing companies. In doing so, a critical mass was formed in the Ottawa Carleton region for a Canadian high-technology nexus known as Silicon Valley North. And there is even a case to be made that the episode had a net benefit for Nortel as well, for in transferring the Intel memory chip technology to Canada, Microsystems played a key role in allowing Nortel to jump ahead of other rivals in the race to develop digital telephone switches.

CHAPTER 5

The Switch to Digital

He was called "Darth Vader"[1]—such was the awe inspired by his technical knowledge, design expertise, and "bloody-mindedness" [2] in bringing new products to market for Nortel during the 1970s. He seemed to be the only one who knew and understood all the pieces, while possessing the requisite toughness to herd a large multidisciplinary team through the process of combining disparate and emerging technologies into a family of first-to-market products.

One thing that contributed in no small measure to his reputation was the way he would sit down with members of his team and challenge them with questions. He wanted to see if they had the passion and drive to get the job done. "Why do you want to do it that way?" he would ask. Then he would pepper them with questions like: "Have you thought of doing it this way?" and "What if this happens?" One had better have all their bases covered when designing for the Darth.

Traditional nine-to-fivers likely found these grilling sessions stressful. If easygoing employees somehow found themselves on the team, they soon realized they had better find work elsewhere. Those who liked to throw themselves into their job as if it were a calling were the kind of people he wanted on his team. These types would welcome, or at least accept, the cross-examinations as opportunities to test ideas and find breakthroughs.

Yet, in his own words, he was "not good at rational management." The egos of those working for him were not always handled with kid gloves. One observer said he was "rough."[3] His passion for getting things done right sometimes boiled over, and voices were raised. Nor was he patient with sloppiness. A transgressor could be the recipient of a stinging rebuke. It was not the stuff of popularity contests, but then there was a job to do. His technical mastery and determination kept team members on their toes; complacency was a rare commodity in his quarters.

Colin Beaumont was the Darth Vader. He played a crucial role in the development of Nortel's digital telephone switches in the 1970s. A photograph taken in the 1990s just before he became one of only four employees (as of the year 2000), to receive the Nortel Fellow Emeritus designation for pioneering a major technological advance at Nortel, shows a friendly smile—not the expected menacing scowl or cranky grimace. A neatly trimmed salt-and-pepper beard covers the lower half of a lean face. Wire-rimmed glasses rest on a nose that looks like it may have taken a bump or two in the rough-and-tumble of the weekend rugby games that he loved to play. On his brow are the creases that often come to persons who engage in long hours of exacting thought.

Beaumont spent his boyhood on a farm in Herefordshire, UK. In his youth, he was one of the teddy boys, a tough lot whose more extreme members scandalized British society with acts of "villainy and thuggery" [4] (the teddy boys were easily recognized by their drainpipe trousers and fondness for rock 'n' roll). But this was just a phase for Beaumont; he later graduated from the University of London with a BSc in mathematics and then went to work for a few years on air traffic control systems. That is where he learned about computers.

In 1964, Beaumont accepted an offer to work at Nortel. Thinking that the capital city of Canada would have some fun things for a young lad to do for a couple of years, he arrived just in time for the culture shock of an Ottawa winter. When spring came, however, things began to look up after he joined a rugby club: the Beavers. That put him in contact with other Brits hired by Nortel during the 1950s and 1960s. To many in this group, the opportunities in Canada were a godsend, a chance to leave behind an environment where even one's accent could be a limitation on career prospects.

Beaumont joined Nortel just as it was launching its drive into computerized telephone switches. This drive got underway with the licensing of the right to make the No. 1 ESS (Electronic Switching System) from Western Electric (the last proprietary product to which access would be allowed under the service contracts, which were then winding down). Coming out of the Bell Labs of AT&T, the No. 1 ESS was a hybrid of old and new technology. The new part involved replacing the hard wiring in the common control unit (the apparatus for managing incoming and outgoing calls) with microcircuits and a stored software program—in effect, a computer system.

With this innovation, the new switches required just a fraction of the floor space, fewer raw materials, and less labor. Any changes, such as adding new subscribers, could be done by simply changing the code of the software program rather than having to rewire. Lastly, it was now technically possible to provide extra consumer services such as call-back notification (a signal that a busy number is now free), speed dialing (one button dials a complete number), and call forward (calls to a number can be directed to another number).

The No. 1 ESS licensing agreement was a valuable headstart for Nortel in the application of computers and stored program techniques to central office switching equipment. It was also a valuable experience for Beaumont, who learned how to design computer systems for telecommunication applications. Several of the old hands at Nortel taught him about telephone switches, and he taught them about computers. All in all, it was good preparation for the projects ahead in which Nortel would be doing its own design.

The first No. 1 ESS to roll off the Nortel assembly line was installed in Montreal for Expo 67. Toronto was next. In all, eleven were installed for Bell Canada over the period 1967 to 1973. Manufacturing the No. 1 ESS, however, was part of a bigger scheme. Nortel planned to modify it for smaller population centers and to learn more about electronic exchanges so that it could do its own designs. The early access to the only functioning model in the world, along with the technical assistance received, pushed Nortel along the learning curve ahead of the many other telecommunication companies in pursuit of electronic switches.

In the mid-1960s, a strategic decision was taken to go ahead with the design of a prototype, what was to be known as the SP-1 (Stored Program-1) switch. It ended up costing $90 million (Canadian) to develop and involved an intensive effort by a team that at times exceeded 100 members. But the gamble paid off better than expected. In Canada, the market penetration rate ended up at 90 percent, and in the US, the

SP-1 switch was a big hit with the independents. Total sales over the period of 1971–1979 were $900 million (Canadian).

While Nortel was able to achieve success in fields such as solid state circuitry by paying top dollar to attract talent from around the world, such was not the case for the development of the SP-1 switch. The engineers who were in the vanguard of telephone switching expertise at AT&T and other companies in the 1960s could not be enticed to work at what was viewed as an upstart operation. What allowed it to happen was a technological discontinuity: the SP-1 was a new kind of switch based upon a recent innovation, that is, computer programs. As such, it was possible to design a switch without having a great deal of experience in the business. All it would take were some people who basically understood how cross-bar switches went together and a group of university-educated youngsters, like Beaumont, who knew about computers.

By the end of the 1960s, Beaumont and other research staff in Nortel and Bell Canada were starting to look at developing a fully computerized version of the SP-1 switch. It would have not only an electronic control system but also equipment for switching voice signals in digital format. With all traffic converted to the binary format of zeros and ones, the telephone system would, in effect, become a giant networked computer. Telephone handsets would function as the input/output devices, while the switches would house the central processing units.

There had already been some conversion of voice signals into digital on the telephone network. Coder/decoder (codec) devices had been developed that sampled the analog waves several thousand times per second. Each of these tiny samples contained a string of binary bits—that is, a sequence of electrical pulses that were either on or off (ones or zeros). Various possible combinations of the binary bits were able to represent different positions in the analog wave. Taking several thousand of these samples every second, the codec device was able to create a good digital replica of the analog signal. At the receiving end, another codec device translated the digital signals back into an analog wave for the ear of the listener.

Digital transmission on the telephone system in the late 1960s was, however, limited to the trunk lines between major central office switches. It was only at this level that the conversion was economical. For lower levels, particularly the "local loop" from the home to the local telephone switch, researchers at the Bell Labs and elsewhere had yet to find a practical solution.

But, in light of ongoing advances in semiconductor memories and logic, research engineers at Nortel and Bell Canada wondered if a practical codec device could become feasible at the local level sooner than expected. Their study, released in January 1969, concluded in the affirmative. This recommendation, however, presented a quandary for senior executives. The SP-1 switch was close to commercial application, and the development of new digital switches would not only carve away resources from the SP-1 but also eat into its sales.

But senior executives at Bell Canada and Nortel had an appreciation that digital systems were just a matter of time and, once on the scene, their advantages would be overwhelming. Digital transmission would facilitate the simultaneous transmission of multiple conversations over one communication path, make it easier to correct signal degradation, and help expand consumer services such as call forwarding and busy-call notification. Another attraction would be an enhanced ability to use the public telephone system to send data messages between computers. So the go-ahead was given for further exploratory study.

This willingness to "cannibalize" product lines surfaces often throughout Nortel's history. It appears to be part and parcel of chasing discontinuities and the process of continuous renewal. If a technology company does not do it to itself, then another company likely will. As John Roth, the current CEO, states:

> If you're going to be cannibalized, it's best to be cannibalized by yourself ... we have to be aggressive enough about attacking ourselves. We think, hey, we've got a great lead, but on the other hand, if somebody's going to challenge our leadership, it should be us, not somebody else.[5]

In 1972, the technological breakthrough came: research staff successfully demonstrated the technical feasibility of a low-cost codec device that would make digital switching practical at the local level. Over ensuing years, BNR would improve substantially on the codec breakthrough, getting costs down much more and increasing capacity. One engineer said that if automobile technology had progressed as dramatically, a Rolls Royce would cost less than $2 and get 40,000 miles to the gallon.

The class of switch selected by Nortel for introducing digital techniques was the PBX sold to corporations. PBXs posed fewer developmental challenges compared to the much larger central office switches on the public telephone network. Moreover, profit margins were higher in the PBX market, which would provide a greater cushion in the event developmental costs overran their budget.

Beaumont had a leading role as a manager in the design of the new digital PBX switch, which was code named SL-1 (Stored Logic-1). But the future Nortel Fellow Emeritus suffered a setback at this stage in his career. The defining moment came at a senior-level meeting at which he did a presentation on the design he had put in place for the SL-1. As he spoke, he could see by the row of expressionless and critical faces that it was not going over well. Sure enough, he found out that the senior managers did not like his approach. They thought it was too ambitious.

Later on, as the SL-1 project neared completion and a promotion did not come his way, Beaumont left the company to work for ITT Corp. in New York. But a year or so after his departure, he was called back by Denis Hall, president of BNR between 1976 to 1981. He asked Beaumont to lead the design of the SL-10, which was a switch for directing traffic on data networks. The SL-10 was one the first Nortel products to break into the European market, and it later formed the basis of the world-leading DPN line of packet switches.

⌗

While the SL-1 and SL-10 switches were under development, planning went ahead within Nortel for the development of digital central office switches. Estimated to be more than eight times as complex as the SL-1 switch, this giant project was raising concerns by early 1975. Specifically, worries were expressed that the research and development tab was going to be much greater than originally forecast and that this would have an adverse impact on Nortel's earnings. It was suggested that development of the family of products should be delayed two or three years.

A task force was formed to look into the issue and make recommendations at a March 6, 1975, meeting of the Policy Coordinating Committee, a tricorporate body comprising representatives from Bell Canada, Nortel, and BNR. After hearing several views, the committee recommended development of the full family of digital central office switches without delay. A deciding factor was a study from Bell Canada estimating a gain of several hundred million dollars if the digital switches could be installed in their network two years sooner.

Once a corporate decision to commit substantial resources was taken, another issue arose. When should the new product line be announced? And what delivery dates should be promised? Like the previous issue of delaying development, it was contentious. Some wanted to announce right away, while others wanted to wait until the product was actually ready.

Executives in Bell Canada and Nortel decided in favor of an early announcement. They were aware that sales of the hybrid SP-1 could be adversely affected, and there was a risk to the company's reputation if promised delivery dates for the new switches were missed. But, in their assessment, the advantages outweighed the disadvantages. One notable benefit was the galvanizing effect of marshaling corporate resources toward a set-in-stone goal. Developing technology products is a complicated process, and the various development teams may get bogged down in discussions over the number and range of features to include. By setting a public commitment to deliver by a given date, a limit would be placed upon the debates.

On the marketing front, Nortel came up with the Digital World campaign, which featured a range of Digital Multiplex System (DMS) switches for all levels of the telephone network—that is digital switches for directing voice traffic at the community (DMS-10), local (DMS-100), trunk (DMS-200), international (DMS-300), and cell phone (DMS-MTX) levels. The campaign was kicked off with three-page advertisements in major trade publications in March 1976. A few months later, the company hosted an industry seminar at Disney World, which was attended by more than 100 business executives from around the world.

After Digital World was approved by the board of directors, Beaumont was asked to head the design team. He had proven himself on the SL-10 project, and no one had yet been found capable of leading the DMS developmental effort. His assignment was to take what had been learned on the SL-1 project and push the boundaries to create a new family of digital central offices switches, subject to the constraint that they retain the principles of "evergreen," reliability, and cost-effectiveness. The evergreen requirement was particularly important: the initial design had to be evolvable so that new versions could be introduced that would be compatible with installed systems. At the time, the computer industry regularly obsoleted vintage generations, so it was a radical departure. This evergreen feature proved to be a key competitive advantage for Nortel.

Beaumont describes the challenge of coming up with new and enduring designs as the "arts of the possible."[6] His first step was to assemble a team combining up-to-date knowledge of engineering and scientific trends with detailed knowledge of conventional systems. Those people with the up-to-date knowledge typically were young people from academe or research organizations; they were the most likely source of new ideas. Those with the knowledge of existing systems were typically the old hands at the company; they were more mindful of market realities and other constraints. The trick was to get the two groups to work together.

Once the team was assembled, it was important to remain "open to ambiguity."[7] That is, the definition of a project in its early stages was not to be made too precise in order to encourage innovation. As an example of ambiguity, Beaumont pointed to the modus operandi of the first president of BNR, Donald Chisholm. The latter defined the goal of the SL-1 switch in rather broad brush strokes as creating the "e-thing."[8] Beaumont believed he had chosen to remain ambiguous in order to challenge, stimulate, and stay open to all the possibilities that could arise. Chisholm apparently was so good at being vague that, in Beaumont's words, "No one knew what he was talking about."[9]

In the later stages of the design project, however, the focus shifted from freedom of exploration to a relentless and single-minded drive to bring products to market. Meeting product milestones and delivery dates became imperative, and the project manager was compelled to decide among several competing design proposals. Once those choices were made, he had to close the door to further suggestions.

The rejection of design proposals was a trial because a large number, including some of the brilliant ones, had to be refused. This was an inevitable consequence of the manager following the basic R&D design dictum that the introduction of new techniques should be confined to a few elements of the product design. For the other elements, it was better to stick with the tried and true as a way to control the risk of design failure.

To balance in the right proportions at the right time two seemingly opposite qualities—the freedom to be creative and the determination to produce tangible results—was, in the words of Beaumont, a "character-building" assignment. In the case of the digital switch project, this was quite evident in some of the interactions he had with members of his team.

One such incident involved Helmuth Krausbar, a manager on the hardware side, and his new recruit, Ernst Munter.[10] The two men were working on a cost-effective and flexible design for some peripheral equipment, and Krausbar arranged an appointment with Beaumont to present their proposal. At the appointed time, the two men walked into Beaumont's office, closed the door and sat down. Munter started to explain the concept in a logical manner.

Shortly after Munter began speaking, Beaumont closed his eyes. Krausbar, who had known Beaumont for many years, knew he was not asleep. It was just a trait—something he did while listening to people. Munter, the newcomer, did not know about this habit so he stopped talking. Beaumont reopened his eyes, and Munter resumed talking. Then Beaumont closed his eyes again, and Munter stopped talking once more. This pattern repeated itself a few times until finally Beaumont had to reassure Munter that he was not asleep. Watching from the sidelines, Krausbar had to suppress an urge to chuckle.

After Munter finished his presentation, and Krausbar had thrown in his two cents worth, the two looked expectantly at Beaumont for his reaction. Quietly, without emotion, his response was: "Good creative thinking guys, but if you mention this to anybody outside this room, you are both fired."[11] His thinking for this area of the system was clearly different. That was the end of the matter, and the two filed out of the office silently. They were so spooked that Krausbar and Munter did not speak about it ever again—even between themselves.

Another meeting had a different outcome, however, and further illustrates the delicate balance between discipline and flexibility. Peter Cashin, a New Zealander who was managing the software team for Beaumont, had become convinced that the development of the DMS switches required a different software design than what was planned. He wanted to introduce a new technique, still unproven in a commercial context, that would permit software modules to be more easily fitted together for the individual configurations of the DMS switches. As well, the new technique would make it easier to develop future generations of the switches that were backward compatible with existing generations (the evergreen feature).

When Cashin and Beaumont met to discuss the design proposal, both were adamant about their positions. Beaumont was resolved to stay with the tried-and-tested approach. He was aware of the merits of Cashin's proposal, but more mindful of the risks inherent in pioneering this new method. He suggested the compromise solution of leaving it, if required, to

a later evolution. Cashin felt, however, that "This was so fundamental that it must be built right at the start, and would be
almost impossible to bolt on later."[12] Continuing to be at log-
gerheads, both men felt their emotions heating up. As the
impasse became more entrenched, frustration and anger surfaced
in the form of raised voices, which deteriorated into a shouting
match. For Cashin there was no going back at this point. He felt
so strongly about the necessity for the new technique that he
would resign his position if it were not adopted. There was no
overt threat to do so, but the implication was there. In the end,
Beaumont relented, and as validated by the passage of time,
Cashin's design proposal proved to be the right one.

The scope of innovation was additionally expanded because
exploratory work and studies did not foresee all the eventuali-
ties that would arise. When Digital World was given the go-
ahead by senior executives, the original thinking was that it
would be a relatively straightforward matter to turn the SL-1
design into a family of digital central office switches. As it
turned out, there were a series of "Oh Hells,"[13] as Beaumont
puts it. That is, the design team discovered several gaps and
incorrect assumptions that forced them into a redesign.

When it came to creating a new design, one of the more
fundamental decisions occurred a year after the Digital World
announcement. This was to assign each telephone subscriber
their own codec line card (for converting analog signals to digital) in the central office switch. This design feature would allow
the service to an individual user to be changed quickly and easily without disrupting service to others. It was a radical departure from the industry trend, one that would be possible only
if the line card could be made sufficiently compact, reliable,
and cost-effective.

Put in charge of this task at the system design level was Jack Terry, an engineer lured away from the UK operations of Marconi Communications Systems in the mid-1970s. By 1979, Terry and his team had created a line card compact enough to fit 640 of them in a standard equipment cabinet, more than doubling the industry standard. The shrinkage was enabled by an integrated circuit: the E13. A product of Nortel's in-house semiconductor facilities, the E13 combined several previously discrete functions into one semiconductor chip. Specifically, filter and other functions were added to the codec device.

While a great design advance, the E13 line cards initially encountered problems operating in the field. A team headed by Krausbar was assigned to get it working. By 1981 they had a new microchip, the E99, that not only operationalized the line card for the field but also brought further advances in compactness and reliability by integrating 27 discrete components. Functions now performed by the chip included control and supervisory functions, such as checking for phones that were off-hook and controlling the ringing sequence.

Not surprisingly then, with the expanded scope of innovation, the project got behind schedule and went over budget. This situation gave ammunition to groups in the organization that were against the whole digital switch idea, particularly those that had their budgets trimmed to hand over resources to the DMS project. In a scene that illustrates why some technology companies fail to adjust to disruptive technologies, Beaumont came under withering attack from these quarters. For his cost overruns, he was nicknamed the Seven Million Dollar Man (after the 1970s TV show). Once again, the question of whether or not to continue with the digital switches surfaced within the company.

For his part, Beaumont was able to show that the products in development would be on the market before anything similar from rival companies. He knew this from what Nortel salespeople were hearing from their customers—AT&T and other suppliers were telling the latter that it would take several years before digital central office switches were ready. This market intelligence thus became an important factor in maintaining support at the senior executive level during "... an exceptionally stressful experience, not one that followed the script."[14] That senior management had the understanding and fortitude to stay with the game plan was, in Beaumont's opinion, a critical reason for the eventual success of the digital switch line.

As the digital central office switching products rolled out into the marketplace, accolades began to pour in. Of note was the receipt in 1981 of the International Industrial Award, the highest honor handed out each year by the Institut international de promotion et de prestige, based in Geneva, Switzerland. Excerpts from the Institute's citation nicely sum up Nortel's achievements.

Northern Telecom [Nortel] has pioneered in many significant stages the development of computer technology in telecommunications, each time setting important technological precedents, such as: the use of stored program control; the development of switching systems controlled by computer software; the launching of a full line of digital transmission and switching systems transmitting with equal quality voice, video, and data signals....

[Nortel] foresaw the convergence of computers and telecommunications, based on the common technology of integrated circuits and software control....[15]

As a result of aggressive cost cutting and the acceptance of Nortel's new products, the fear of a drop in earnings in the 1970s from rising research and development expenditures never materialized. In fact, earnings rose steadily every year between 1970 and 1979—from $5 million to $111 million (Canadian). This increase of 2,200 percent was the best performance in the telecommunications equipment industry. Revenues went from $0.5 billion to $1.9 billion (Canadian), nearly a 300 percent rise over the decade. By 1979, the workforce had increased by one-third to 33,300, and spending on plant and equipment was up nearly fourfold to $702 million. Research and development stood at 7.1 percent of revenues in 1979, compared to 4.6 percent in the early 1970s.

In the PBX market, Nortel's SL-1 switches were just so much better than competing products that they easily moved to the top of customers' shopping lists. By the end of 1978, over 300 of these switches had been purchased by major US corporations. An early convert was CitiCorp Inc., which paid $2.5 million in 1976 to purchase and install Nortel's PBX system for its office complex, turning thumbs down on the option of leasing a system from AT&T affiliate New York Telephone Co. In pursuit of PBX business, Nortel displayed an "aggressiveness uncommon in the telecommunication industry"[16] according to the *Wall Street Journal*. The departure from the traditional conservatism of telephone companies was said to be a reflection in part of the policy of recruiting executives from other industries, which began with the hiring of John Lobb in 1971.

In the central office market, Nortel began by picking up business from the independent telephone companies in the late

1970s. The agreement with Continental Telephone Corp. for a shipment of $50 million worth of digital switches in the summer of 1979 was a early breakthrough. Shortly after, Central Telephone and Utility Corp. signed a $70-million agreement for DMS-10 and DMS-100 switches. Other customers were US military organizations—for example, the US Air Force placed a $23 million order. Finally, not to be overlooked among the early adopters were AT&T's new rivals in long-distance telephony, particularly MCI, which took $24 million worth.

But the biggest plum was getting a foot in the door with AT&T itself. With Department of Justice and Congressional inquiries into AT&T's alleged anticompetitive behavior in progress in the early 1980s, the telephone giant was under pressure to give the appearance of not being a closed system. As well, Nortel's marketing approach was persistent: the company set up a sales office next to AT&T's purchasing depot, and over the course of two years, Nortel's lawyers, technicians, engineers, and other specialists attended hundreds of meetings with their AT&T counterparts to ensure compliance with AT&T's numerous specifications. The end result was success: in 1980, AT&T approved the lower end of Nortel's digital switches for purchase within the Bell group (later followed by approval for higher-end switches).

In 1982, AT&T awarded Nortel a four-year contract worth $200 million to supply DMS-200 switches. Later the same year, the New York Telephone Company became the first AT&T affiliate to buy Nortel's central office digital switches. The order, following a two-year trial, was for more than $150 million worth of DMS-100 switches spread over four years. Even AT&T's manufacturing arm, Western Electric, subsequently got into the act, licensing the DMS-10 switch to add to its range of products.

The floodgates were now opening wide. Within two years of the divestiture, twenty-one of the twenty-two former Bell operating companies were clients of Nortel. David Vice, president and chief operating officer of the Canadian operations at the time, recalls what it was like:

> When the divestiture took place, we found that our customers embraced us in a bloody bear hug. They'd been with AT&T and Western Electric all those years and had been taken for granted. They hadn't been treated like customers. All of a sudden, along we came with the technology and at least the appearance of knowing how to help them cope with the competition they were going to face. We were the supplier that was going to help them modernize their networks. They just took us in. We were a hit.[17]

While nearly every other company in North America was struggling merely to hold its head above water in the recessionary economy of the early 1980s, Nortel was going from success to success because of its superb positioning in telecommunication technology and markets. Besides offering the only digital switches available at the time of the AT&T breakup, Nortel was just about the only independent equipment supplier offering products with the same operating procedures and quality standards as the US Bell companies. This was due to the 1970s process of developing the DMS product line in conjunction with Bell Canada, a former branch of the once tightly knit AT&T family. And the link with Bell Canada paid off in another way—as a showcase for DMS switches in action.

Surfing a tidal wave of demand, Nortel had urgent requirements of its own: the speedy and massive expansion of its research facilities and manufacturing capacity. Major corporate financings, such as several issues of preferred shares in the first half of the 1980s, were required. However, thanks to double-digit annual growth in sales, much of the expansion could be

financed by plowing rising cash flow back into the company.
Together, these internal and external sources of financing led
to an increase in spending on plant and equipment to $2.4 bil-
lion (Canadian) in 1985, up from $702 million (Canadian) in
1979. The research and development budget enjoyed an
increase of similar proportions.

Much of the expansion in the first half of the 1980s was
into the United States in support of the penetration of that market. A major addition in 1980 was the manufacturing plant and
research facility in Research Triangle Park near Raleigh, North
Carolina. In 1984, another one million square feet was added,
doubling the size of the flagship facilities. There were several
expansions into California: a business communication plant in
Santa Clara, a research lab in Mountain View, and an electronic
chip-making plant in Rancho Bernardo. Atlanta, Georgia, was
the location for a transmission-manufacturing facility.

Over the period 1979 to 1985, Nortel's annual revenues
marched without interruption from $1.9 billion to $5.8 billion
(Canadian), a 200 percent increase. Although not progressing
as smoothly, annual earnings finished the period much higher
too, rising 260 percent to $411 million (Canadian). In turn, the
price of Nortel's stock soared. The period from mid-1982 to
mid-1983 was quite amazing: investors bid up the share price
almost without pause—resulting in an appreciation of some
250 percent over the twelve months.

6

The Dance of the Regulators

Until 2000, Nortel operated as the subsidiary of a larger corporation. In the early years, Bell Canada and Western Electric owned nearly all the shares in the company. This ownership arrangement lasted for well over half a century, changing only in the late 1950s when the consent decree signed with the US Department of Justice motivated Western Electric to sell its stake to Bell Canada.

Bell Canada (later BCE Inc.) then owned a 100 percent interest in Nortel, which it maintained until 1973, when it slipped to 90 percent after the public bought several million shares of Nortel's IPO. Additional listings of stock, including several on foreign stock exchanges, reduced Bell Canada's equity stake even further, down to about 55 percent by 1982. Further dilution brought ownership close to 38 percent by the end of the 1990s.

As a subsidiary, Nortel enjoyed considerable immunity from market forces. Until the middle of the 1990s, Nortel was a preferred supplier to Bell Canada, which gave it the right of first proposal. That is, it had the right to submit bids to supply the carrier's equipment needs before any other supplier. In exchange, Nortel promised not to sell equipment at a lower price to other companies.

Bell Canada not only provided Nortel with a guaranteed market but also lent support to its drive into research and development by contributing financially to BNR. Bell also provided important data, such as technical requirements and customer specifications, and served as a testing ground for prototypes. Thus, although Nortel had lost its link with Western Electric, the remaining relationship with Bell Canada turned out to be even more salutary, giving the subsidiary a solid platform for a new life as an originator of product designs and manufacturing processes. Some analysts have even suggested that without the link to Bell Canada, Nortel would not likely have succeeded.

Nortel could not have picked a better corporate parent. Beside being one of the largest corporations in Canada with deep pockets, Bell Canada operated as a regulated monopoly. Under legislation restricting Bell Canada's rate of return on assets to a prescribed markup over its costs, profitability was assured—although the trade-off for security in income was a restriction on how high it could go. The result was that the telephone utility nearly always enjoyed a strong cash flow from its telephone operations, a cash flow that would be available for building up unregulated subsidiaries such as Nortel. The setting was about as secure and supportive as it could get. The special relationship between Bell Canada and Nortel was therefore a critical behind-the-scenes factor in the development and marketing of the digital switches that revolutionized telephone networks from the 1970s onward.

Yet, right from the beginning of Nortel's quest for technological supremacy, Canadian government agencies, focused on other priorities to be sure, were threatening to tear down the special relationship between Nortel and Bell Canada. For various reasons, they believed that the vertical integration of the two companies was not in the public interest and that Nortel should be divested from Bell Canada. The assault, stretching out over the mid-1960s to the mid-1980s, consisted of several investigations that could have aborted the Nortel story before it fully unfolded. A sword of Damocles, as it were, was suspended by a thread over the whole endeavor.

It was not always so. Government agencies posed little threat for well over the first half of the century. They adopted a kind of laissez-faire stance that was supportive in many respects. This was particularly true of the Board of Transport Commissioners, the agency that reviewed applications for rate increases (until it was superseded by the Canadian Transport Commission in the mid-1960s). As part of that process, it heard presentations from the private sector for and against the rate increases.

A complaint sometimes heard in this context concerned Bell Canada's relationship with Nortel, which had been described as unfairly restricting trade and foreclosing markets in the telephone equipment market. But in several rulings over the years, the Board of Transport Commissioners decided that Bell Canada's relationship with its unregulated subsidiary was beyond their purview. The regulatory framework was thus benign for the Bell Canada–Nortel axis for many decades.

A highlight of the charitable treatment received at the hands of regulators occurred in 1963 when the Industrial Wire and

Cable Company, a competitor to Nortel in the manufacture of wire and cable, applied to the Board of Transport Commissioners to have Nortel severed from Bell Canada or alternatively merged with the telephone carrier whereby it would fall under regulatory review.

The initiative from Industrial Wire and Cable, quite ingenious in concept, contended that Bell Canada's ownership of Nortel was illegal, that according to Bell Canada's founding charter of 1880, the telephone company was allowed to hold shares only in "proprietors of lines of telephonic communication."[1] And Nortel did not appear to be a telephone company as such—indeed its letters patent precluded it from owning telephone systems. Therefore, Bell Canada would have to either dispose of its subsidiary or fold it back into itself in order to comply with the original charter.

Bell Canada's defense was even more ingenious, claiming that upon incorporation, Nortel purchased from Bell Canada a single line of telephone wire running between its plant and Bell Canada's headquarters in Montreal. The line sent messages in one direction only and was maintained by Bell Canada, but was still nonetheless owned by Nortel. Over the years, as both companies moved to new premises, the location of this line changed, but it was still maintained.

As such, Nortel, so the telephone lawyers argued, was a proprietor of a telephone line and thereby qualified to be a subsidiary of Bell Canada. The defendants also argued that Nortel was not in violation of its letters patent because no service to the public was offered over the single line. Nortel was not a telephone carrier—it just owned a telephone line. Upon what might seem to be the narrowest of technicalities, the case was dismissed, some 20,000 feet of telephone wire settling the issue.

This case was just about the last hurrah of the era of friendly overview on the part of government officials. A change in attitude was signaled when a team of investigators from the Royal Canadian Mounted Police (RCMP) obtained search warrants and raided the executive offices of Bell Canada and Nortel on November 29, 1966. Their purpose was to gather internal company documents for an inquiry under the *Combines Investigations Act*. The director of investigations and research, located in the Bureau of Competition Policy within the Department of Consumer and Corporate Affairs, initiated the inquiry. He had come to the conclusion that the vertical integration of Nortel and Bell Canada was being used to push the latter's monopoly into unregulated segments of the telecommunication sector. As such, the two companies would be in violation of section 33 of the *Combines Investigations Act*, the section that makes it illegal to form or operate a monopoly "to the detriment or against the interests of the public."[2] His goal was to obtain evidence in support of his belief.

The decision to investigate was prompted by a stream of complaints over previous years about Bell Canada and Nortel foreclosing important markets to competitors. The complaints basically fell into three categories. The first involved competitors claiming that they were in a disadvantaged position against Nortel because the latter could rely upon the tremendous resources of its parent to wage ruinous competition. In this regard, it was alleged that Bell Canada was cross-subsidizing its manufacturing subsidiary by paying higher-than-market prices for its telephone equipment purchases.

A second kind of complaint, although more of concern to government regulators, was the potential for Bell Canada to use Nortel as a tool for circumventing regulation; for, in allegedly paying higher prices on equipment bought from its subsidiary (and through other subtleties), Bell Canada could transfer profits out of the regulated section of its accounts to the unregulated side. As such, the interests of telephone subscribers would not be protected as intended.

A third category of complaint centered on the charge that Bell Canada was extending its monopolistic position into unregulated sections of the economy by acquiring independent telephone companies and then having the newly acquired companies switch their purchases of telephone equipment to Nortel. And once snatched away, the former supplier of equipment stood little chance of winning business back because of the preferred relationship Nortel had with Bell Canada.

It was one of these so-called market foreclosures that triggered the combines inquiry launched in 1966. Bell Canada had gone on an acquisitions binge in the 1950s and early 1960s, gobbling up many independent telephone companies. This consolidation was said to have been triggered by General Telephone and Electronics (GTE) Corporation (the largest independent telephone operating company in the United States) taking over some telephone companies in Canada. Bell Canada did not want GTE to get too big a toehold in the Canadian market, so it launched an acquisitions program of its own.

Things came to a head in August 1966 when Bell Canada made an offer to buy out two telephone companies: Maritime Telegraph and Telephone Company in Halifax and the New Brunswick Telephone Company in Saint John. The takeover would be arranged by getting the Board of Transport Commissioners to approve the issue of 1.2 million Bell Canada common shares to swap for shares in the two maritime companies. The premier of Nova Scotia, Robert Stanfield, was incensed over the attempt to take control of the telephone utility in his province. That the provincial utility would be compelled to drop its existing equipment supplier and buy from Nortel was anathema to him.

When attempts to negotiate a compromise solution broke down, Stanfield recalled the Nova Scotia legislature from a recess and passed amendments curtailing the voting rights of shareholders in the provincial telephone company. This meant that even though Bell Canada would own 51 percent of the shares once the deal went through, control of the corporation would be denied. A few days later, the Board of Transport Commissions in Ottawa approved the issue of the 1.2 million Bell Canada shares required to complete the acquisition, although control of the company did not pass over after the swap since the shares were nonvoting.

Concurrently, Stanfield filed complaints about Nortel's purchasing practices with the director of investigations and research in Ottawa. It was the last straw. The string of earlier complaints could no longer be overlooked now that a provincial premier was on the warpath. An investigation would have to be launched.

The inquiry prompted Bell Canada and Nortel to commission a group of economists to do a study of the telecommunication industry and policy issues. The studies were put together into a book *Telecommunications for Canada: An Interface of Business and Government*,[3] edited by economics professor H. Edward English. Coming out in 1973, some three years before the combines unit was to publish findings from their lengthy investigation, the book took the lead and set the tone in the policy debate.

One thrust of the economists' arguments was that vertical integration with Bell Canada would enable Nortel to become a strong competitor in foreign markets. In providing a guaranteed level of sales, the preferred-supplier arrangement would enable Nortel to get its unit costs of production down to internationally competitive levels. Moreover, Bell Canada could, through BNR, help finance the costs of developing leading-edge telecommunication products with export capability. In short, a laissez-faire approach would enable the Canadian telecommunication group to become an instrument of industrial development for Canada, creating a home-grown research and development complex, as well as a viable manufacturing company.

The studies in Professor English's book also addressed the allegation that Bell Canada, by reputedly paying high equipment prices to Nortel, was siphoning off monopoly profits from the regulated telephone market. Evidence was provided that the contention of excessively high prices was simply not true. Indeed, it was found that prices tended to be lower than comparable items sold in the open market. This was seen as consistent with the clause in the preferred-supplier agreement stipulating than Nortel furnish equipment to Bell Canada at prices no greater than those charged to other customers.

As for the complaint of extending monopoly by acquiring telephone operating companies and making them switch their equipment purchases to Nortel, it was argued that Bell Canada was more or less forced into the acquisitions because US competitors GTE and Continental Electric would have done so and compelled the Canadian telephone companies to buy from their preferred suppliers. Thus, Bell Canada's acquisitions binge provided assurance that more of the domestic telephone industry would remain Canadian owned, a kind of National Policy (that is, state protection) without the politicians.

In December 1976, the director of investigations and research for the *Combines Investigation Act* finally released a summary of the findings in a report entitled *The Effects of Vertical*

Integration on the Telecommunication Market in Canada.[4] The report decried Nortel's dominance of the equipment market in Canada, which was estimated at 70 percent of total sales. The report attributed this commanding position to Bell Canada's procurement policies favoring Nortel. The conclusion was that the Bell Canada–Nortel relationship was not in the public interest and that it should be severed. The recommended approach for divestiture was to have Bell Canada distribute shares in Nortel to Bell's shareholders.

The findings of the report from the *Combines Investigations Act* inquiry team were blasted at the time by Bell Canada officials. The immediate reaction of Bell Chairman Jean de Grandpré was that the report was outrageous and had reached a "stupid conclusion."[5] A few days later, the chairman reportedly stormed angrily into a senior level meeting at the Department of Consumer and Corporate Affairs, called the report garbage, and demanded that it be withdrawn. On leaving the meeting, he said to the minister: "I'm going to Europe, and when I come back in ten days, I expect the report to be withdrawn and thrown into the garbage can, where it belongs."[6]

His entreaties were to no avail. The report of the director of investigations and research had recommended that the Restrictive Trades Practices Commission (RTPC) should carry out public hearings into the arrangement. Some days after de Grandpré's return from Europe, the RTPC announced that it would launch a public hearing into the question of whether the relationship between Bell Canada and Nortel was in the public interest.

The RTPC panel traveled coast to coast, making stops in urban centers to collect testimony and submissions. Attendance was sparse. Lawyers representing the combines investigation branch at the hearings claimed that the poor turnout was due to Bell Canada putting pressure on witnesses to stay away, threatening not to do business with them if they registered complaints. The claims were investigated by the RCMP and dismissed. The road show continued for another four years, crisscrossing the country several times. Attendance rose and, by the end, in 1981, the commission had heard from over 200 witnesses, studied more than 2,000 exhibits, and compiled a 35,000-page transcript of proceedings.

De Grandpré was feeling quite frustrated throughout the RTPC hearings. He declared that the uncertainty created by the inquiry was handicapping Nortel in its efforts to market its new digital switches in world markets. Customers in those markets would feel more secure about buying the Canadian product if they knew the supplier was not at risk of losing its supporting partner. He added:

> We were not just fighting our competitors or interest groups, but our own government. I don't understand their stupidity. They want winners, but they want to destroy one when they finally get one.... It doesn't speak highly of their intelligence.[7]

De Grandpré's level of frustration was surely exacerbated by the more aggressive stance of the Canadian Radio and Television Commission (CRTC), the government agency that took over in 1976 from the Canadian Transport Commission the job of overseeing applications for telephone rate increases. Now there were two hounds nipping at the heels. In one ruling, the CRTC loosened Bell Canada's monopoly by allowing interconnection to its telephone network (which had happened several years earlier in the US market).

More serious was the issue of "integrality," the growing integration of income and costs from the regulated and unregulated operations of Bell Canada. Such a comingling of financial flows made it difficult for regulators to carry out their assigned task said CRTC officials. Were telephone subscribers subsidizing the expansion of the telephone company and its subsidiaries into new unregulated markets? And were they getting their fair share of the profits?

In the late 1970s, the CRTC decided that answering these questions required bringing Nortel under its regulatory scope. The first major ruling in this regard concerned the treatment of the $185-million (Canadian) profit that Bell Canada and Nortel would earn from winning a giant contract to provide Saudi Arabia with an advanced telephone system. The CRTC rejected a proposal from Chairman de Grandpré to split the profit equally between shareholders and subscribers, instead deciding that all of it was to be treated as regulated income. Furthermore, the CRTC pegged the rate of return at 15 percent on Bell Canada's equity investment in Nortel, seeking, in their words, "to protect telephone subscribers from the potential burden of having to cross-subsidize continuing capital expenditures."[8]

Executives at Bell Canada and Nortel looked upon this latest turn of events with alarm. Indeed, they now saw the CRTC as a greater threat than the RTPC and its inquiry into vertical integration. At the time, Nortel was in the process of trying to sell its digital switches in the United States, and that push required spending huge amounts of money to expand manufacturing and research capabilities. A newly invigorated regulatory body, the CRTC, was, in pursuit of other social objectives, undermining the ability to finance those expenditures.

It was too much for the Bell Canada executive team. After an appeal to the prime minister and his cabinet ministers came to naught, Chairman de Grandpré embarked on a major reorganization of Bell Canada as a way to preserve the ability to work with Nortel and its other subsidiaries. In April 1982, Bell Canada applied to the Department of Consumer and Corporate Affairs to annul its parliamentary charter and bring the company under the *Canada Business Corporations Act*. This allowed Bell Canada to set up a holding company called Bell Canada Enterprises Inc. (BCE) that would hold the regulated Bell Canada and Nortel as subsidiaries. Shareholders were informed that the reorganization would empower BCE to make investments without being subject to government restrictions or prohibitions. They were further told that the reorganization was not subject to CRTC approval.

The CRTC nevertheless announced that it would hold public hearings on the matter, starting in February 1983. It hired three consultants to prepare reports and to make recommendations. The three submitted their reports independently just before the hearings were to start. They all advised the CRTC to oppose the reorganization because it did not remove incentives to cross-subsidize and because it curtailed the commission's ability to execute its regulatory function.

Within days of submitting their reports, however, the consultants sensed a sudden and mysterious change in atmosphere inside the CRTC, a feeling reinforced when the three were abruptly relieved of their consulting duties. The CRTC, working to a tight schedule, released its recommendations in April 1983. The report, in a word, was a capitulation. The commission concluded that "managerial flexibility is particularly necessary...at this stage in time. As Canada proceeds into the information age, its future as an industrialized state will depend heavily on high-quality managerial, technical, and research skills such as those found within the Bell group of companies."[9] In other words, the view that Bell Canada and Nortel were emerging as instruments of industrial development had won the day.

Just as the CRTC was staging a retreat, the RTPC report on vertical integration came out. The main conclusion was that "competition in the telecommunication equipment market… in much of the world is highly restricted," and that the market security afforded Nortel through vertical integration "provided it with some breathing space to engage in expensive product development." Therefore, the "evidence in this inquiry does not establish that, on balance, the separation of Bell Canada and Nortel would improve performance in the telecommunication equipment industry or in the delivery of telecommunication services by Bell and other carriers."[10]

With two government agencies agreeing to leave the Bell Canada and Nortel nexus free to pursue their corporate plans, the path was cleared for Nortel to emerge as a technology superstar. The sword of Damocles, hanging by a fraying thread over the whole enterprise, was snatched away before it could fall, and a collective sigh of relief emanated from the executive offices of the Canadian telephone conglomerate. Attention could now be turned to getting on with the business of breaking into new markets and creating growth.

If successful, the implications for the Canadian economy would be beneficial—higher employment and capital formation. In place was a kind of covert industrial policy that evolved out of the private sector and was subsequently sanctioned by political leaders—a scheme for economic development that perhaps had far better results than the conventional approach based on government subsidies and industrial strategies concocted by state planning agencies.

7 Going Global

Technological excellence, pricing, and service usually clinches a sale at home, but in foreign markets that is often not enough. Many other factors can enter into the sale besides the features and price of the product itself. It could be a simple side deal that includes export-import financing assistance from a government agency, or it could be a more complicated matter involving such things as commitments to build local manufacturing and research facilities.

In the early 1980s, a main challenge facing Nortel was to sell its portfolio of digital products into new markets around the world. For a company that had virtually no marketing department for most of its existence, this would be no small feat. Nortel might have had some great gadgets to sell, but the company was still a relative newcomer when it came to dealing with customers in foreign markets. As it turned out, this hurdle was cleared easily, and Nortel's history offers several interesting stories on the intricacies of penetrating foreign markets.

A first order of business was to find a replacement for John Lobb, who retired in 1979 from the chief executive position at Nortel's US subsidiary. So Light, Scrivener, and de Grandpré (who was also chairman of Nortel around this time) hired a professional executive search firm. A few months later the name of Edmund Fitzgerald was put forward. When contacted by de Grandpré, Fitzgerald said he was not interested.

But Light knew Fitzgerald through the Electrical Manufacturers Club (a forum for telecommunication executives) and the board of directors at Inco Ltd. Light got Fitzgerald to have dinner with de Grandpré in Montreal; Fitzgerald may have gone intending to have no more than a nice weekend in the cosmopolitan ambiance of the Quebec city, but as the dinner at the prestigious Mount Royal Club wore on, he discovered that the prospects for Nortel were too compelling to let pass. He agreed to become the president of Nortel's US subsidiary, starting in early 1980.

Fitzgerald came from a wealthy and prominent Milwaukee family with interests in shipbuilding and insurance. He had trained as a mechanical engineer in the 1940s and served as a commanding officer of a marine detachment aboard the US Navy flagship *Mount McKinley* during the Korean War. He was tall and solidly built and had a shy personality tempered with a folksy sense of humor. One observer described him as a person who made friends easily.

During the 1970s, he was chairman and chief executive officer of the family-owned business, Cutler Hammer, which was a provider of electronics products to the US military. In 1978, his company was taken over by a Cleveland manufacturer of automobile and truck parts, Eaton Corp. After a year of serving on the executive of his new employer, Fitzgerald exited as planned. He was in this ensuing state of quasi-retirement when he found himself wined and dined by de Grandpré.

What de Grandpré and Light liked about Fitzgerald was that he had connections in the right places. "Ed Fitzgerald was of the industrial elite in the United States,"[1] said de Grandpré. Fitzgerald belonged to most of the major business and trade associations in that country, usually serving as chairman or a director. These included the Committee for Economic Development, Conference Board, National Electronics Manufacturing Association, and the World Economic Forum. As such, Fitzgerald was on friendly terms with many Fortune 500 CEOs, a valuable asset for spearheading sales of PBX and central office switches into the United States. He would be a kind of traveling salesman for Nortel south of the border. He would put a much-needed American face on the Canadian upstart.

In addition, he was well connected politically, having spent several years in Washington, lobbying to snare defense contracts for Cutler Hammer. And he was a member of several Department of Defense advisory committees and President Reagan's National Security Telecommunication Advisory Committee. He knew his way around Washington, and with strong ties to the Republican administration, he would be an effective spokesperson for Nortel.

⌗

Edmund Fitzgerald is also the name of the ship that sank without a trace in a nasty storm on Lake Superior in the mid-1970s, a marine disaster that was immortalized by folksinger Gordon Lightfoot in the popular ballad, *The Wreck of the Edmund Fitzgerald*. The largest ore carrier on Lake Superior at the time of its launch in 1958, the ship had taken its name from Fitzgerald's father, who owned the Milwaukee shipbuilding company that had built it.

Upon his arrival at the headquarters of the US subsidiary, Fitzgerald saw the corporate equivalent of another marine disaster about to unfold—one in need of immediate attention. It was brought on by the 1978 acquisitions of several office equipment companies: Sycor Inc. and Data 100 Corp. (both companies were pioneers in the business of designing and manufacturing data entry, facsimile, and word processing systems for office networks).

The troubles started with the departure of key entrepreneurial executives, perhaps spurred by Lobb's heavy-handed style. By one count, seventeen senior people had left in the first year. It also became apparent that there was some unexpected rot: Data 100 product lines were discovered to have higher production costs and more obsolete models than originally expected. It appeared as if Nortel had bought into a kind of high-tech Edsel. The products, which were based on networks created within mainframe and minicomputer environments, were on their way to extinction because of the arrival of microcomputer networks.

Fitzgerald set to work at getting the people down there to understand the Northern culture. He also decided that the US operations had to pull back substantially from the diversification into office equipment and refocus resources on the company's forte in digital switches. Two Data 100 plants were closed down, and a line of computer disk drives was chopped. A total of $220 million (Canadian) in special charges was taken to cover inventory write downs, bad debts, staff reductions, and the extinguishing of the unamortized value of the acquisitions. The end result was Nortel's first annual loss in over a decade.

The US subsidiary of Nortel returned to profitability in 1981, and so did Nortel as a whole. Fitzgerald's reorganization helped stem the financial drain of a misdirected foray into electronic office products just as sales of digital switching products in the United States skyrocketed upward (Nortel's annual sales jumped 25 percent). In May 1982, Fitzgerald was promoted from the top job at the US subsidiary to president of Nortel (Light, preparing for retirement, moved over to the chairman position). Fitzgerald's promotion was a reward for turning around the US situation, but it was also an appointment to give him higher status within the company so that he would have more leverage doing the rounds in the United States. The chances of success would be increased if Nortel fully donned an American face and appeared to be as much a part of the US economy as possible.

⌗

Fitzgerald was instrumental in smoothing the way for Nortel's expansion into the US market, particularly when it came to providing air cover in the political arena. In 1980, he had set up a public affairs office under the direction of Norman Dobyns to lobby the Department of Commerce for permission to classify Nortel's US operations as a US company. Once so defined, exports of the US unit would be eligible for credits from the US Export-Import Bank, thereby increasing its competitiveness in foreign markets (by being able to offer US government-funded loans to prospective clients). Since companies that were 20 percent or more owned by foreigners could not be classified as US companies, Fitzgerald sought a special ruling to obtain an exemption.

This exemption was eventually granted because of the company's growing US workforce (then approaching 13,000) and its huge investments in manufacturing plants and research facilities. But in the fall of 1981, the lobbying for an exemption was temporarily superseded by a more pressing matter: the passage in the US Senate of Bill S898. This legislation, seeking to update the 1934 regulatory framework of the telecommunication industry to modern realities, called for a restructuring of the AT&T system to permit more competition in the carrier and manufacturing segments.

One section of this new bill was quite alarming to Nortel. It authorized the FCC to formulate rules to secure reciprocal treatment of US telecommunication firms in foreign markets—rules that would allow the regulatory board to limit, even bar, imports from countries that did not allow the same access to domestic telecommunication markets. Nortel, having the preferred supplier arrangement with Bell Canada, could therefore find itself completely shut out from the US market.

But that was not all. The bill contained two other threatening measures. First, the FCC would be empowered to deny certification to any equipment that had more than 50 percent of its value produced in a country not meeting reciprocity conditions. Second, AT&T, which would be compelled under Bill S898 to adopt a fair and nondiscriminatory procurement policy, was expected to pressure the FCC for permission to rule out bids from manufacturers having 20 percent or more foreign ownership.

If the Senate bill was approved by the House of Representatives and President Reagan, Nortel would obviously be dealt a crippling blow. It had invested heavily in new technologies and an extensive corporate infrastructure. To be shut out before it had a chance to recoup these costs would have not only confined Nortel to the minor leagues, but perhaps even jeopardized the company's very existence. It was, therefore, imperative to deal with the political threat. Responsibility for navigating these tricky shoals fell to Fitzgerald.

In the early 1980s, protectionist sentiment was on the rise. The deficit in the US balance of payments was widening to record levels, and a chorus of US corporations was complaining loudly about foreign competitors grabbing market share. Exports from Japan were a big concern, especially in the automobile industry. The major gains scored by Japanese vehicle manufacturers against General Motors, Ford, and Chrysler were alarming to many. In this kind of environment, Fitzgerald and the public affairs office of Nortel went to work on Capitol Hill to get the reciprocity clauses removed from the telecommunication legislation before it was passed into law.

Staff from Nortel's US subsidiary individually canvassed the twenty congressmen on the subcommittee handling the bill in the House of Representatives. They met regularly with their specialists and attended every subcommittee hearing throughout the spring and summer of 1981. Nortel also went public by getting articles published in the press, doing presentations to trade associations, and writing letters to members of congress. The main message was that congress should consider the impact of the reciprocity clauses on the 13,000 US citizens working for Nortel. The company, in short, was saying that it was different than an Asian exporter since it was contributing directly to US employment and capital formation.

In an appearance in front of a House subcommittee on March 3, 1982, Fitzgerald elaborated on this theme. He mentioned that most of the jobs created by Nortel were high-quality jobs, especially the 1,200 positions in research and development. Of the $880 million sales in the US market in 1981, approximately 90 percent came from the company's US plants. Furthermore, the largest portion of company assets were now in the United States—46.5 percent versus 45 percent in Canada. Lastly, the US investment community owned 32 percent of Nortel stock. Overall, the picture presented was of a model US citizen, of a corporation so integrated into the US economy that any damage to it would be deleterious to the US economy as well. It was a very persuasive argument to be sure, but not one certain of success considering the fact Nortel had no facilities in any of the constituencies of the subcommittee members.

What helped decide the issue in Nortel's favor were the speeches in late 1982 by candidates running for the Democratic presidential nomination. In expressing support for protectionist measures and reciprocity clauses, they stirred President Reagan and his Republican administration into action on the issue of free trade. As part of his campaign, Reagan sent the US trade representative to a House subcommittee to convey disapproval of the reciprocity clauses, implicitly conveying the message that he would exercise his veto power to kill the protectionist bill. To allow the bill to pass would likely have provoked a global trade war since reciprocity clauses had been banned under the General Agreement on Tariffs and Trade (GATT).

Nortel breathed a sigh of relief when Bill S898 died in the House. However, two years later, in 1984, another version of the reciprocity clauses appeared in a proposed trade bill, and Fitzgerald was back in front of a congressional committee. He argued that such protectionist measures were misguided as they did not address the root cause of the deficit in the trade balance. Other factors were more important, such as the dramatic appreciation in the value of the US dollar. Reciprocity clauses were just hunting licenses that would not ensure a level playing field. With the help of his testimony, the second trade bill was defeated, and Nortel thereafter enjoyed a degree of freedom from political threats in the United States for the rest of the 1980s.

⌗

One of Nortel's biggest achievements was to be the first foreign company to make major inroads into the Japanese telecommunication market. The breakthrough was announced in December 1985, a time when Japanese manufacturing companies were running circles around US counterparts. The flow of exports was virtually one way, with ever-rising shipments from Japan piling up on the wharves of North America. Corporations in the United States and Canada were feeling beleaguered, and a feeling was taking hold that Japan was an invincible juggernaut. But swimming against the tide was Nortel.

Nortel had started the sales campaign way back in the 1970s, trying to sell digital switches to the world's second-largest telephone company, Nippon Telegraph and Telephone (NTT). Bids were submitted, but NTT officials told the Canadian ambassador to Japan that there would not be any business to hand out. It was the same story for any foreign company wanting to sell to NTT, which at the time was a state-owned monopoly buying nearly all of its equipment under long-term contracts from four favored domestic suppliers.

Not surprisingly, NTT became a source of trade friction between the United States and Japan in the early 1980s. The Electronic Industries Association was one body lobbying to have NTT's practices put on the table at the GATT multilateral negotiations. When the Japanese government balked at including NTT, the GATT talks halted. The flames of protectionism were fanned, and reciprocity clauses surfaced in telecommunication bills brought before the congress in the early 1980s.

With events pointing toward a full-blown trade war in which companies such as Nortel could be shut out of the US market, Fitzgerald attempted to do something about the impasse between America and Japan. As chairman of the Committee for Economic Development, a policy organization made up of chief executives from major US corporations, he organized a joint meeting with the association's Japanese counterpart in March 1982. At a meeting in Hawaii, both sides aired their views and looked for ways to defuse the situation. Fitzgerald frankly told the Japanese delegation that he believed their telecommunication market had some of the worst trade barriers.

After the meeting, Fitzgerald was back at work at Nortel when he received an invitation to visit the Japanese ambassador to the United States. At the meeting, he once again repeated his view that NTT was a major sore point in trade relations. The ambassador responded with another invitation, this time to visit the head of NTT, Hisashi Shinto, to discuss the possibility of making a sale or two. The two men agreed that if a deal could be made, it would be good not only for Nortel but also for US-Japan trade relations, since it would demonstrate that Japan was open for business.

So Fitzgerald flew over and met with Shinto. The latter said NTT would place orders as long as the products supplied were compatible with Japanese specifications, conformed to strict quality standards, and were delivered on schedule. Fitzgerald responded by setting up a Japanese subsidiary to explore opportunities. To head Northern Telecom Japan Inc., he selected Gordon Tagasaki, a former classmate who had worked for Fitzgerald as a consultant.

Teams from Nortel and BNR went to Japan to learn more about Japanese technical standards, while teams from NTT reviewed Nortel's equipment capabilities. It was a laborious process that went on for at least a year and a half. Start-up costs were estimated to be as high as $60 million. A loss-leader contract was signed to provide a small transportable telephone switch for emergency situations. To fill the order, the DMS-10 switches were modified so that they could be hooked up with the Japanese telephone network.

All the sacrifice and hard work started to pay off in late 1985, when a memorandum of understanding was signed with NTT for the supply of $250 million worth of DMS-10 switches, the first major contract awarded to a foreign firm by the Japanese telecommunication giant. The contract would extend over seven years, with shipments starting in 1987. Competitors—four Japanese suppliers and AT&T—were unsuccessful in winning the contract largely because they did not have a switch to fit the low-end niche that the DMS-10 served.

A formal purchase agreement was signed in the spring of 1986 after NTT certified that the DMS-10 could be safely connected to its system. Two rivals, AT&T and Rockwell International, kicked up a fuss when they learned that Nortel had applied to obtain financing from the US Export-Import Bank. Fitzgerald justified this application by pointing out that the switches were to be exported from the Raleigh plant in North Carolina and that NTT was anxious to buy the switches from the US plant in order to help alleviate the US trade imbalance. If they bought them from Canada, that would not address the critical trade issue. The Reagan administration turned a deaf ear to the complaints and supported Nortel.

Big things were hoped for in the Japanese market—in fact another replay of the US boom was envisioned. The expected upsurge in sales would be a timely one, coming just as the US market was starting to level off. Additional contracts did come, such as those from Japanese companies for PBXs and from NTT for the DMS-200 switch to be used as a backup on the congested Tokyo network. But overall, the business garnered was not a groundswell such as that experienced in the US market.

It was nevertheless quite a coup for Nortel—to be the first foreign company to make major inroads into the Japanese telecommunication market. The company had leading-edge products to be sure, but a critical success factor was having Nortel take an American guise with Fitzgerald at the helm. As chairman of a high-level committee in the United States, he was able to establish contacts with key Japanese people and position Nortel products as "Made in America." Thus, the digital switches satisfied not only a technical requirement to upgrade the Japanese telephone system but also a political imperative to defuse tensions over trade issues.

✤

Ian Craig joined Nortel in 1967. Earlier, he had received his bachelor degree in electrical engineering from the Imperial College in London and was working at a British computer firm when Nortel made him a salary offer he could not refuse (this was not hard to do since there was a wage freeze in place in the United Kingdom at the time). After a few years developing electronic telephone sets in the research labs of Nortel, he transferred over to the marketing side. His skills with anecdotes and golf clubs were some of the personal assets that helped him climb the ranks of the marketing division at Nortel. By the time of his retirement in mid-2000, he had reached the top position of chief marketing officer.

One of his more important assignments came in 1985, when he was asked to be the managing director of the fledging UK operations. The original reason for the assignment was to win a supply contract from British Telecom, but just days before his departure, it was awarded to another company. There did not seem to be any point in going, but he was told he had to go anyway and just make the best of it.

Fortunately, one of those discontinuities that Nortel is so fond of exploiting was just starting in the British market. A number of alternate carriers, such as Mercury Communications, were being formed in response to a loosening of regulations, presenting Nortel UK with more opportunities to sell its wares. Craig spent the next two years working this new market, achieving key breakthroughs. During his stint, Nortel's sales went up fivefold, from $10 million to $50 million per year.

The business was won through a combination of initiative, adroitness, and serendipity. On his first approach to Mercury, Craig found that the chief executive officer, Gordon Owen, would barely give him the time of day. Owen had a set-in-stone deadline for cutting a new network into service, and he did not want to risk missing it with an unknown equipment supplier. He asked Craig why he should go with Nortel when he already had a supplier whose top guy he could call in case things needed to be fixed quickly. "I know him," he said, "I can call directly to the top and get any resource I need to get this project done."[2] Craig offered to do the same, to give him direct access to Nortel's chief executive, but there still was uncertainty in the Mercury quarters.

It came right down to the wire. Sitting in his office Friday afternoon, Craig got a call from Owen, who said, "If you can take a million dollars out of the contract, there is a very good chance you could go away a happy man."[3] This was no small request, since the bid was for $19 million, with a $15 million penalty attached for nonperformance. Craig thought of contacting his superior, the manager of the European operations, to get permission to alter the contract. But he did not think he could reach his boss in time since he was traveling in the Middle East. Moreover, his boss had been a Bell Canada man, where the culture was more conservative, and Craig believed he would have a hard time sanctioning such a large price reduction and penalty clause.

So he acted on his own. He knew he could recoup the cost reduction on "the hedge"—that is, if Mercury was willing to pay in US dollars (which its parent company Cable and Wireless had), Nortel could avoid the costs of the currency hedging operations that would be required to protect contract payments against a devaluation in the pound. That same afternoon, he walked onto Owen's office and laid a revised contract on his table. It provided for a cost reduction of three-quarters of a million dollars if payment could be made in US dollars. Another sweetener was the offer to carry spare equipment so that Mercury would not have to incur the costs of carrying the items itself. Owen picked the contract up and looked across to a fellow executive, who nodded. Owen then turned and said, "Mr. Craig, you've just won the business."[4]

Craig went back to his office. He was so exhausted from getting the contract ready that the euphoria did not set in until the next day. He rang up his financial officer and his superior to tell them that Nortel had won the contract but that he had to give substantial concessions. Their reactions were less ecstatic. On the following Monday, however, his deal was vindicated when Mercury called back and raised its order to $39 million. Profitability, which had been doubtful under the original terms, went through the roof because the overhead costs could now be spread over a much larger volume of business.

Nortel UK assembled a project team and put together a system, cutting it into service on the day of the deadline. Having proven itself, Nortel UK won many more contracts from Mercury, sometimes just on the basis of a telephone call. One day, for example, Owen called up and asked Craig whether he had an international switch. Craig replied that he did have one—the DMS-300. One with 1,000 trunk lines was subsequently shipped over. Mercury liked it enough to order several more, for a total of $6 million—all done over the telephone.

Another day, Owen asked Craig about Centrex. Craig described how it provided PBX and other services to corporations from the central office switch of the telephone carrier. He then put together a proposal, which Owen examined. In a car with Craig on the way to a NFL exhibition football game in Britain, he leaned over and said he would like to get the Centrex. By the time they reached the parking lot of the stadium, the requirements had been ironed out, and Craig had a deal.

The order for a Centrex was another instance of serendipity for Craig because it got him out of a jam on another front. Earlier, he had ordered a DMS-250 switch for a customer on the basis of a letter expressing a desire to purchase one. When the switch arrived, the customer reneged and left Nortel UK with a choice between carrying the switch in inventory or of returning it to the factory. He decided to hang onto it, following the practice of Nortel's US operations. Like them, he thought, it would be useful to have an inventory in order to speed up delivery to the customer.

In Nortel's European operations, however, such inventories were not allowed. Indeed, when company auditors came across it, Craig was "written up with black marks."[5] He was preparing to write a rebuttal to the report when the order came in from Mercury for a Centrex, which Craig was able to quickly fill by changing the software program in the DMS-250. Thus, once again, Craig turned lemons into lemonade.

And then he turned lemonade into champagne. The established telephone giant in the UK market, British Telecom, became concerned that Mercury had Centrex services while it had none. They worried that their rival now had a competitive edge. British Telecom then approached Nortel UK and placed a large order for their Centrex service. And once a relationship was established with the entrenched carrier, Nortel received follow-up business in other areas.

Following his stint in the United Kingdom, Craig worked on several assignments in North America until 1992, when he was transferred back to the managing director position of the UK operations. Shortly after, he got a promotion to the managing director position for all of Europe. His responsibilities would be a lot more weighty this time around, since Nortel's presence in Europe had expanded substantially since his last visit.

Of particular note was the acquisition of STC (Standard Telecommunications and Cable) PLC, a British electronics firm, in 1991. The latter was indeed a significant step for Nortel. It cost $4.4 billion, which was financed in part by issuing $1.7 billion in long-term debt (raising the portion of debt in Nortel's capitalization structure to approximately 50 percent). Of specific value to Nortel were STC's fiber-optics expertise and existing customer relationships with British Telecom, Mercury Communications, and other European telecommunication firms.

Craig's return to Europe was another piece of good timing. A wave of demand for telecommunication equipment was building as a result of the deregulation of European telecommunication markets. In the United Kingdom, the big change was the removal of restrictions that had kept cable TV companies from competing for business in the telephone industry.

To focus on developing business among UK cable TV companies, Craig set up a sales force under Ron Patterson, the project manager who had performed well on the initial contracts with Mercury. In addition to their technologically advanced products, the Nortel sales force had another factor in its favor: the image presented by the AT&T and Western Electric team. Its effort was spearheaded by employees from the United States, while Craig, Patterson, and others on the Nortel team were British in origin. At parliamentary dinners and other events, Craig and his coworkers could easily join in the conversations on cricket, royalty, and other uniquely British matters, while the Americans "were left out of it."[6]

Selling to the cable TV companies turned out to be a completely different prospect. In the telephone industry, there is exhaustive analysis of requirements and a range of precise specifications with which to comply before winning a contract. The cable TV industry was far less formal, as Craig found out when dealing with Telewest, a joint venture between a telephone and cable company. To get to know the head of the joint venture, Larry Carleton, Craig invited him to a round of golf. Carleton was just learning how to play, and Craig helped him with some of the finer points of the game.

A little while later, Telewest put out a tender for equipment and received several bids, including one from Nortel. The telephone people in the joint venture wanted to do an exhaustive study of the proposals, but Carleton, who was from the cable industry, told them he wanted to do business with somebody he liked and trusted. Craig was in Europe at a conference when he got the call from Telewest. Over a pay telephone at the Nice airport, he was given ten days to meet ten conditions. It took him a few days longer, but he still got the business. The experience was quite a contrast from the telephone industry, where deals could take over a year of meetings.

Once Craig discovered the personal nature of business dealings in the cable TV industry, and the preference for timely delivery, he worked it for all it was worth. He invited more cable TV executives to golf courses and other venues to get to know their needs, and to promise the speediest delivery and installation of switches. The reward was several more contracts, often agreed to in the strangest of places One deal was arranged in the washroom of a golf club—quite a contrast to the boardrooms of the telephone industry.

But the personal approach to selling had its occasional pitfalls. In an outing to the Ryder Cup, Nortel had given one cable executive an electronic security card to gain entry to the hospitality tent. Somehow, though, a few forgeries had gotten into the batch of cards that Nortel had purchased from the contractor, so when the executive swiped his card through the security machine, it set off an alarm. Police were going to take him aside, but he somehow eluded their grasp and escaped into the crowd. On the lam, he found a phone on the grounds and placed an irate call to Nortel staff to come and rescue him. Matters were eventually set straight. And despite being a fugitive from the law for a few moments, the executive later did sign with Nortel.

❄

When the memorandum of understanding was signed between Nortel and the Chinese state planning commission in June 1993, Nortel's CEO, Jean Monty, was ecstatic. The potential for sales was clearly immense. Chinese plans called for a major expansion over the 1990s of its still-underdeveloped telephone system. At the signing ceremony, Monty equated the scope of opportunities in China to Nortel's opportunities in the US market of the 1980s.

Shortly after signing the memorandum of understanding, some big deals were finalized—over $100 million worth of DMS-100 and SuperNode switching systems were sold to three provinces. The switches would (in some cases) be developed jointly and would be put in place according to a rather aggressive schedule of eighteen months. Later in the fall, switching equipment worth $160 million was sold to four other provinces.

More good news came in the fall when a bill was introduced in the US congress to relax restrictions on telecommunication exports to China. The *Commercial Export Restriction Act* would overhaul limitations on the transfer of technology to China and other communist countries put in place a few years earlier. Nortel applauded the legislative initiative as it would free its US subsidiary to move into China. Nortel would now be able to use all its resources to play catch-up with the European telecommunication firms that had earlier entered the Chinese market unencumbered by government restrictions.

For the next year, there was a gold-rush atmosphere in China as North American companies poured in to get a piece of the action. In the fall of 1994, the Canadian government organized a trade mission to China, led by Prime Minister Jean Chrétien. By the time it was over, Nortel had announced a deal to sell $350 million in telephone equipment to China. Much of the equipment would be made in plants in China once Nortel carried out plans to boost its Chinese work force to 4,000 people over the next three years.

Nortel afterward worked on implementing its commitment made in the 1993 trade agreement to invest over $130 million to construct research and manufacturing operations in China. One highlight in this regard was the creation in 1995 of a joint venture called Shenyang Nortel Communications Co. Ltd., with the Liaoning Posts and Telecommunications Scientific Research Institute. It would manufacture and sell fiber-optic transmission equipment.

Although Nortel was going ahead with its investments, big orders from Chinese customers at this stage were starting to trail off. There were a few announcements of deals over 1995, but the amounts were either small or not mentioned. In the annual meeting with shareholders in April 1996, Nortel's CEO, Jean Monty, revealed that China was proving to be a tougher market to crack than expected. "There is significant competition, and the incumbents in the market have been fighting back," he noted.[7] He also pointed to delays in receiving official authorizations for contracts as part of the reason for performance in China being below expectations.

Other companies were encountering the same difficulties. An executive with a Calgary oil firm said the experience of setting up an office in China was a real eye-opener. "I knew it would be difficult, but as far as the frustration level is concerned, I probably missed [estimating] it by a factor of ten. As a place to do business, China is difficult: it's the most difficult and frustrating place I've ever worked. My advice is not to come to China unless you have a very long-term view. Because it is very time-consuming and very expensive."[8] Examples of the cost were: $40,000 import duty levied on his Volvo car, rent of $10,000 a month for a modest three-bedroom apartment, and $5-per-minute long-distance calls to North America. Bureaucratic hoops and hurdles tried the hardiest souls, contract laws were weakly enforced, and bribery was said to be necessary at times.

A Nortel official in China lamented cutthroat competition from the rising influx of foreign companies, a competition that at times had the air of a barroom brawl as companies clambered over each other to get business. He said: "It's extremely competitive. You really have to beat out the other guy. Everyone here is trying to undercut each other. Everyone is trying to get a piece of the pie."[9]

⌗

In 1994, another spot of trouble arose on the foreign front when the Canadian Minister of Trade, Roy MacLaren, revealed that the US subsidiary of Nortel was being denied US government export assistance in its bid to win a $1.3 billion telecommunication contract in Saudi Arabia. Meanwhile, a bid from AT&T for the same contract was backed by US government export credits.

Under article 1102 of the North American Free Trade Agreement, both Canada and United States had agreed to make export promotion assistance available to foreign-owned companies operating in their countries. Counting on this commitment, Nortel was submitting the bid for the Saudi Arabian contract through its US subsidiary because the DMS-10 switches in question would be exported from its plant in North Carolina. It was also advantageous for the corporation to present itself as a US company because Saudi Arabia owed the United States a debt of gratitude for being rescued from the clutches of Iraq in the Gulf War.

AT&T had for years lobbied to exclude Nortel's US subsidiary from eligibility for US export aid, ever since the latter had broken into the Japanese market with the help of US government export credits. AT&T's pleas fell on deaf ears in the Reagan and Bush administrations partly because Nortel's chief executive officers, Fitzgerald and Stern, both had close connections with the Republicans. But when the Clinton Democrats came to power, AT&T's pleas were heard loud and clear. An early sign of a shift in attitude at the presidential level was an order to have the Nortel telephone switch at the White House replaced with a switch from AT&T. The substitution later got Clinton in a bit of hot water on Capitol Hill since the AT&T equipment was brought in without tender.

Next, it was announced that Nortel would no longer be eligible for US export credits. A report from the office of the US trade representative provided the justification: Nortel was to be denied export assistance on the grounds that the Canadian telecommunication market was closed to US suppliers by virtue of the preferred-supplier agreement between BCE and Nortel.

Roy MacLaren, the Canadian Federal Trade Minister, disputed the reasoning in a letter to the US trade representative. He claimed that the preferential arrangement was a matter between two private companies and therefore not an appropriate subject for the trade report (which was supposed to deal with just restraints of trade arising out of government practices). Furthermore, it was argued, the claim that US companies faced barriers to trade in Canada was inaccurate, as substantiated by AT&T's recent multimillion dollar equipment sales to Unitel Communications, BC Telephone Company, and Manitoba Telephone.

In a matter of weeks, the trade dispute was resolved. Nortel would be taken off the list of companies ineligible for US export assistance in exchange for BCE and Nortel immediately ending their preferred-supplier arrangement. In a sense, the arrangement was an antiquated thing. Nortel had emerged as a supplier of advanced telecommunication equipment and did not really need the help of a business agreement to win contracts from its parent company or any other company for that matter. With the markets of Latin America, Asia, and Europe expected to be a vital source of corporate growth in years ahead, it was far more important to have access to US financial aid selling into those foreign markets.

Attention next shifted to the Saudi contract. The competition was fierce, but Nortel looked like it was in the driver's seat. It was undercutting the AT&T bid by about $300 million. In addition, much of the contract involved the upgrading of equipment originally put in place by Nortel (as a consequence of BCE winning some big contracts to set up telephone systems in Saudi Arabia during the 1970s and 1980s).

Nortel's chances, however, evaporated when US President Clinton and his state secretary began to lobby the Saudis in favor of AT&T. The campaigning included a personal letter from the President to King Fahd. With AT&T identified as the quintessential American company, Saudi Arabia's obligation to buy American in the wake of the Gulf War clearly pointed in the direction of AT&T. Not surprisingly, therefore, AT&T won. In international trade, it is often politics, not economics, that rules.

8
CHAPTER

Full Speed
A Stern

Paul Stern, chief executive of Nortel from 1989 to 1993, cut a distinctive figure in the drab conformity of corporate America. His preference for European suits, French-cuffed shirts, and fast sports cars set him apart. So did his ability to communicate in five languages and his sensitivity to cultures outside the United States. He had an aura that might have captured the eye of a casting director on the lookout for a debonair agent 007 in a James Bond movie.

Contributing to the impression was a square jaw, steely gaze, and "the appearance of a supremely confident, self-directed man,"[1] as one interviewer noted. However, another interviewer observed that he was "brimming with a confidence that approaches braggadocio,"[2] an impression that may have been reinforced when Stern revealed he felt way underpaid even though he was earning a salary of $1.4 million.

Actually, he may have been right about being underpaid. The résumé of Paul Stern is one of the most impressive anyone will ever see. It shows an impressive string of achievements and a rapid progression through the ranks to the top echelons of the top corporations. The son of an American diplomat, Stern was born in 1938 in Czechoslovakia. His family moved from place to place, living in exotic locations such as Northern Africa and the Middle East. Stern's childhood was marked by a tragedy: the death of his father. His mother, fortunately, was a strong individual. She took her family to Mexico where they prospered under her wing. Her children received a good education—her son Paul went to the American High School in Mexico City and then to prep school in Boston.

Growing up in so many different countries, it was natural for Stern to become multilingual. He became fluent in English, Spanish, and German, and was able to get along in Italian and French. In his twenties, he went to university and earned several degrees. By the time he was finished, his academic credentials included a bachelor in electronic engineering, a master's in science, and a doctorate in solid-state physics (the latter was completed in 1966 at the University of Manchester).

After university, Stern's career took off when he joined IBM Corp. There his language skills got him assigned to trade missions outside the United States, where he rubbed shoulders with senior IBM executives. This closeness to the top paid off when, a mere four years into his employment, Stern landed an executive position in corporate finance.

He continued to climb the hierarchy of the corporate world by exceeding the expectations of his bosses and jumping ship frequently. After IBM, he accepted a senior position with West German consumer products giant Braun AG, becoming its chief operating officer within four years. Next came senior management positions at defense manufacturer Rockwell International and computer company Burroughs Corp. of Detroit.

When Burroughs acquired rival Sperry Corp. in 1986 and renamed itself Unisys Corp., Stern worked closely with chairman, Michael Blumenthal, to integrate the two companies. As the first president of Unisys, Stern was in charge of reducing overlap and costs, an unpleasant task that involved laying off thousands of staff.

Stern was assumed to be Blumenthal's successor until the executive team that ran Unisys was expanded from four to seven persons, a reorganization that left Stern's influence diminished. Feeling that his path to the top was blocked, Stern resigned in 1987. His wounded pride was assuaged by a $6.7-million severance package. With no real need to work, he retired from corporate life to pursue personal interests and be with his family in Pennsylvania.

The next year was spent enjoying a relaxing routine of tennis, painting, and travel. Stern also wrote a book on the topic of getting ahead. Called *Straight to the Top*,[3] the publication contained advice for those who aspired to ascend the corporate ranks. Coming from someone whose own corporate career could easily be described as a textbook case, one might say that Stern was eminently qualified to expound upon the subject.

In his book, Stern advises would-be corporate-ladder climbers that they need a burning, ever-present, desire to get ahead. To advance rapidly, he recommended creating a unique image, such as he had with his European fashions and fast cars. His other important points were: do not be afraid to drop hints that you will leave if not challenged and rewarded; take responsibility for managing your boss; and train yourself not to be afraid of getting fired.

Once in the management ranks, wrote Stern, the would-be corporate-ladder climber needs to keep in mind that the more demanding they are as supervisors, the more respect they will get. What matters more than being right or wrong is being decisive. Lastly, whether you are a manager or not, remember that there is no such thing as corporate loyalty and that money is not everything, but it is quite far ahead of whatever is in second place.

✠

While Stern was writing his book and enjoying the easy life, Nortel's chief executive, Edmund Fitzgerald, was thinking about retiring. When his thoughts turned to finding a successor, they zeroed in on Stern. The two men had met previously at the Electrical Manufacturers Club, an organization where the elite from corporate America got together twice a year for a weekend meeting. The two also had served together on President Reagan's National Security Telecommunication Advisory Committee on Trade.

Fitzgerald saw Stern as being sufficiently well connected in Washington to be able to carry on his own work of lobbying US politicians to secure Nortel's place in the American market. There was always the threat that trade regulations would be amended to exclude Nortel from the lucrative US market or that export aid would be cut off for products shipped from the company's US plants. And Stern did have the connections. Besides sitting on a number of high-level government committees such as the Defense Policy Advisory Committee on Trade, he had worked on fund-raising committees for President George Bush.

Fitzgerald also liked Stern's international background and experience with acquisitions. If Nortel were to reach its goal of $30 billion in revenues by 2000 (as outlined in Vision 2000, a corporate goal formulated in 1987), the company would need to make several acquisitions in foreign markets to produce the required 15 percent a year growth in revenues. In addition, it would be necessary to arrange joint ventures with several foreign players in the telecommunications sector.

The penetration of foreign markets was seen as one way to generate the growth that would give Nortel the scale and R&D capability to meet the competitive threat posed by large and growing rivals. Moreover, Fitzgerald saw it as an effective response to the European telecommunication giants that were entering the North American market through acquisition. First there was Alcatel's purchase of the telecom operations of ITT in 1986 and then Siemens's purchase of the telecom subsidiary of IBM in 1988. Rather than wage a merely defensive battle against the new competition in its core market, Fitzgerald thought Nortel should also take the fight to the backyards of its foreign rivals.

Finally, Fitzgerald wanted Stern as his replacement because of his reputation as a demanding executive who would not be afraid to push through tough cost-cutting measures. In 1988, Nortel's revenues had grown by 10 percent, but its expenditures in the areas of selling, general, and administration grew by 16 percent, and research and development grew by 21 percent. Operating profit consequently fell 18 percent compared to the previous year, and Fitzgerald and the Board of Directors felt the time had come for Nortel to bring its cost structure back under control. Otherwise, the company would lose its position as one of the lowest-cost producers in the telecommunication equipment industry.

In opting for Stern, Fitzgerald was passing over the company's top six executives who reported to him. In a sense, he was just maintaining the tradition at Nortel of hiring a chief executive from outside the company or from the parent company, Bell Canada. But it was more than just tradition. He was also concerned that the engineering backgrounds and lack of worldwide experience of the six executives would limit them. The chief executive, he felt, should be someone with enough pull in Washington to carry on work there, as well as someone who possessed a demonstrated toughness for presiding over a shake-up of the corporation.

As Stern had left Unisys vowing never to work for another company again, Fitzgerald had to reel in his man slowly. He first offered Stern a seat on the Nortel board of directors and a consulting contract. Stern took the bait in April 1988. In this consulting position, he helped Fitzgerald map out a program for streamlining operations and consolidating assets. Announced in early December 1988, the centerpiece of the program was a $200-million charge to cover the layoff and relocation of up to 2,500 staff—5 percent of the workforce.

Besides getting spending under control, another objective of the restructuring was to get the company out of product lines and projects that had become "commoditized." For example, it would be more economical to buy printed circuits from Asian exporters rather than to continue to make them in-house at the plant in Belleville, Ontario. Other facilities affected by the restructuring were the transmission facility in Quebec and the network support services in New Hampshire.

Fitzgerald was right in his hunch that Stern was too ambitious a person to stay retired. When he offered the chief executive position to the fifty-year-old Stern, he accepted and assumed the office on March 1, 1989. Fitzgerald would remain on as chairman until his retirement the following year. With Stern in the lead, the two men would implement the restructuring they believed the company needed. The two were in high spirits during a press interview arranged at the time of the succession. Stern joked, "My wife says, 'Thank Ed for getting you out of the house.'"[4] Sticking with the spousal theme, Fitzgerald replied, "My wife has a list of things for me that she's been preparing for forty-two years."[5]

☩

With his reputation as a no-bull, cost-cutting boss, Stern's arrival on the scene sent bolts of fear through the ranks. Rumors swirled around in the coffee rooms and in the hallways about where he would strike. The stories, told in hushed tones, were juicy blends of fact and fiction. "Did you hear?" someone would say, "Stern fired a top vice president." Another would add, "He has put an entire plant on the block in Ontario," and yet another would declare, "Stern says he has never seen a company where people travel so much—so now we will all be going coach."

For the first six months of his term, Stern went on a whirlwind tour, visiting company operations in far-flung corners. He shook hands, smiled a lot, and tried to calm nervous employees. But his purpose was more than to put a human face on the reorganization—he was also asking questions, collecting facts, and assessing the situation in preparation for his next move. And it looked like it would not be a comforting one. He told one reporter, "I am sad to say there are still pockets of mediocrity in this company. And I don't tolerate mediocrity."[6]

One site included in his tour was BNR in Ottawa, where he warned a group of engineers that he intended to cut back on basic research and make it more market-orientated. The visit ended abruptly when one engineer rhetorically asked Stern if the famous patent-a-day Bell Labs in New Jersey would have discovered the transistor in 1948 had it done away with basic research. It was a revealing incident, an early indication of the perils awaiting anybody attempting to change the organization and culture.

During the first year of his term, Stern presided over the implementation of the $200-million downsizing plan announced before his arrival. A number of plants were closed. Pie-in-the-sky projects were trimmed out of the research budget. It was a shame that so much money had been poured down the drain on them, but to continue throwing good money after bad would be even more of a travesty. These projects were "a lot of slop" in Stern's words, unlikely ever to result in marketable products.

On the Washington front, Stern looked to his connections to hire a vice president who would be responsible for developing business with US defense and intelligence agencies. Stern saw institutions such as the CIA and National Security Agency as needing to send and receive more and more information over vast distances. To further establish credibility within the defense and national security establishments, Stern appointed former US defense secretary, Frank Carlucci, to Nortel's board of directors.

After his first six months of touring and information gathering, Stern began work on a major reorganization of responsibilities at the senior executive level. By the time it was completed in 1991, Nortel had seven divisions. A key feature of the internal realignment was a decentralization of management, of distributing executives geographically to meet the challenges of globalization. With these sweeping changes, Stern wanted the corporation to become more sensitive to local customer needs, to gain control of Nortel's somewhat wayward regional operations, and to alleviate the warring tribe syndrome.

Three global product divisions were established, along the lines of the company's three major business lines: public networks (central office switches), private networks (PBX systems and data switches), and wireless (mobile phones). Each was to have an operating president and global mandate to ensure that product portfolios were comprehensive, integrated, and met the needs of every market. Four regional marketing divisions were established, also headed by presidents. These marketing divisions would be headquartered in London for Europe, Tokyo for Asia, Nashville for the United States, and Mississauga for Canada.

These and other changes were unsettling. Over half of the two dozen corporate officers on staff in 1989 departed, retired, or were reassigned. Vacancies were often filled by people from outside the company. Some observers worried about the years of experience that had gone out the door, and noted that morale was sinking throughout the corporation. Stern, of course, was only trying to gain control of the corporate reigns in order to carry out the strategies he believed were necessary. To do so, he needed loyal lieutenants in key roles. But the way the process was handled did not seem to help his cause.

He operated more like the brilliant loner, dominating meetings with his grasp of the problems and the putting forward of solutions. He liked to act decisively and did not spend much time building rapport. Those personally affected by the changes were often not warned beforehand of what was to befall them. The experience of John Taylor, group vice president for transmission products, was illustrative. When his responsibilities were folded into other divisions, he said it "...came as a surprise. No one had discussed it with me."[7] He subsequently left.

In late 1991, a few months after the restructuring exercise was complete, Stern turned his attention to improving company morale. Surveys conducted by an opinion survey firm had confirmed deep-seated unhappiness among the rank and file. Stern took a step toward addressing the situation at a meeting of his top managers. He told them, "We are not doing well on internal communication [we need] a sense of pride in what we do rather that the negativism that exists in many quarters."[8]

For his part, Stern sat down with one of his vice presidents, John Strimas, to map out a massive motivational initiative known as "Journey To Leadership." The centerpiece was a campaign-style swing through Nortel, starring Stern himself. It consisted of a series of appearances at selected Nortel facilities, with Stern flying in from headquarters on the corporate jet. His inspirational speeches on core values and goals would be the high note in a week of plant-wide festivities that included marching bands, cheerleaders, and balloons.

⌗

In October 1989, Nortel outlined a new vision called FiberWorld, which promised a line of access, transport, and switching products for fiber-optic telecommunication networks. The products had been under development for three years under the leadership of David Vice, president of Nortel from 1985 to 1990. They were expected to incur further developmental costs of $1 billion over the next decade as prototypes were refined and made ready for the market.

Fiber-optic systems, to be phased into telecommunication carrier networks over the course of the 1990s, would have capacity and speed many thousand times that of traditional copper-based telecommunication systems (as such, fiber-optic systems would be called broadband networks while copper-based systems would be called narrowband networks). Company studies projected that as traffic rose over communication networks, the market for fiber-optic equipment would be $15 to $20 billion per year by the late 1990s (an estimate that was not far off). Clearly, there was a lot of growth potential for any company in a position to supply this market.

Nortel's new product line was the first on the market to incorporate a recently created international standard for high-speed fiber-optic networks, called SONET (Synchronous Optical Networks). This standard would promote compatibility of equipment from different vendors, allowing customers to purchase from a variety of sources. Analysts estimated that Nortel had up to one full year lead on its rivals in this market. Once again, Nortel had scooped its competition, being the first to market with new products at the forefront of a major trend in telecommunications, just as it had done earlier in 1976 when it announced Digital World.

The FiberWorld products included the successful DMS family of products, which were upgraded to the new standard. These new versions consisted of the S/DMS TransportNode (which transported long-distance signals), the SuperNode (which acted as bridge between narrowband and broadband networks), and the AccessNode (which delivered signals over the local loop to the customer). These products were to be introduced to customers over the next two years.

After the announcement of the new line of fiber-optic products, Nortel share prices jumped nearly 5 percent. Investors were intrigued with the potential of broadband systems, which would not only allow telecommunication carriers to handle rising volumes of traffic but also enable new and exciting services such as movies-on-demand. As it turned out, the move into fiber optics helped launch the Internet.

⁜

When Stern assumed the mantle of chief executive in 1989, the PBX telephone market was saturated. Price discounting was rife, and profit margins were under pressure. Nortel, the top supplier in the world market with the largest installed base (over 8 million lines) of digital PBXs, was about the only company with profitable operations—although just barely. This superior performance was due to domination of the large end niche, where Nortel's strength in providing valued-added features (such as call forwarding, least-cost routing, conferencing, voice mail, and so on) was winning the battle.

Competitive pressures in the PBX market eased in the early 1990s when AT&T replaced the executive in charge of its PBX business line. Profitability on Nortel's offerings, sold under the Meridian brand name, was also enhanced by the marketing of two new additions to the family. One was the Meridian Norstar, the first PBX to bring advanced telephone set features to the small business environment. The Norstar sets had programmable keys and liquid crystal displays providing feature status and user-friendly instructional prompts. It was a modular system whose eight main lines could be expanded to 128 ports—an important selling point for small businesses that were expecting to grow in future years.

The other addition was the Meridian-1. It was based on a fully customizable and modular architecture capable of servicing thirty to 60,000 lines—more than twice the capacity of the nearest competing product. A key element was the ease of adapting the product for sale in other countries: instead of a laborious process involving hardware changes, simple alterations to a software program would make the product consistent with varying technical and regulatory standards around the world.

Both new varieties of the Meridian line were very successful. Nortel's 1992 Annual Report noted that over three million Norstar telephone sets had been shipped to more than sixty-five countries. The Meridian-1 had more than 18 million lines in use worldwide, making it the most widely used digital PBX anywhere. Clients of the latter included Banque Nationale de Paris, British Telecom, the Kingdom of Jordan, Kuwait Oil, the US Postal Service, and the US Air Force.

In the 1990s, research and development staff continued to work on turning the PBX into much more than a device for switching telephone calls. Under-the-skin application modules were developed to provide a variety of value-added PBX functions. Nortel had a particular edge in application modules for voice mail (Meridian Mail), Automated Call Distribution (Meridian Max), and host-link support (Meridian Link). Another advance was the introduction of Asynchronous Transfer Mode (ATM) and other broadband switching interfaces that would permit desktop videoconferencing as well as high-speed connectivity with data networks. Yet another advance was integration of the computer and telephone sets so that control of telephone operations—ranging from answering to transferring a call—could be transferred to personal computers.

In 1992, Nortel launched the VISIT product, initiating several field trials and kicking off a marketing effort with a product demonstration at the trade fair COMEX Fall '92. VISIT turned the personal computer into a personal call management center, letting users dial, log calls, set up directories, and track usage. It delivered real-time video pictures of the persons on the other end of the line and let participants in their different locations work together concurrently on the same spreadsheet or computer file.

While PBX systems were the largest component of Nortel's enterprise networks products group (generating over half of the revenues) in the early 1990s, another significant chunk of business communication revenue came from the Data Packet Network (DPN-100) product line. This was a family of packet-based switches used exclusively to route data traffic over private and public networks between computers.

With the development of the DPN-100 switches, Nortel had emerged as a pioneer in the area of data communications—its specialty being transmission over wide area networks (WAN), those networks that connect local area networks (LAN). The early start and technological lead were parlayed into domination of the WAN niche; the switches were known to be more flexible, have faster recovery, and yield up to 30 percent cost savings. Given Stern's background in computers, it was natural for him to target this niche for growth, especially in Europe where his connections and multilingual skills made him feel at home.

With their clear superiority and Stern's focus, the DPN-100 switches spearheaded the penetration of foreign markets and industry sectors in the early 1990s, establishing a beachhead from which other product lines could be sold. A notable contract win in 1990 provided 300 DPN-100 nodes to the largest data transport network then in existence: SITA, the Paris-based global telecommunication organization of the air transport industry. Another megadeal for the nodes was signed in the same year with Air France for its reservation system. Financial institutions, such as the Society for Worldwide Interbank

Financial Telecommunication (SWIFT), were big customers, using DPN-100 for electronic transfer of funds. UPS and other large courier companies purchased the product for their systems of tracking deliveries.

In 1990, Nortel was one of the first to market a more advanced packet switch that took advantage of the changeover from analog to digital networks. Offered under the name of DataSpan, it was based upon the frame-relay mode, which promised improved data transmission performance by relaying a packet directly to its destination instead of terminating and restarting it at each network node as did the X.25 standard for communicating across systems. As such, it did not require checking functions at each node and so it was faster.

✻

As 1992 wore on, reports began to surface in the press that glitches in Nortel's DMS switches were likely the cause of some network failures recently experienced at US regional telephone companies. The interruptions and delays in fixing the problems prompted senior telephone executives in America (according to more than one source) to take the unusual step of complaining directly to senior executives at Nortel's parent, BCE. They let their displeasure be known in other ways, too. Some of the US regional telephone companies delayed acceptance of the switches and software upgrades they had ordered, postponed orders, or even shifted their business to alternative suppliers.

Nortel's software predicament had arisen in part from an attempt to win customers by cramming a large number of features into its DMS switches (e.g., call forwarding and call waiting). To do this, the company had put the underlying software through several rewrites over the course of a decade, ending up with over 24 million lines of customized code. Nortel still had the best product in terms of value-added services, but growing complexity meant that upgrades required increasingly more time and resources.

Also slowing down the process was the greater number of tests that had to be performed to ensure that changes in one place were consistent with code elsewhere. The extra tests were not always enough to catch every bug, as the experience of the regional telephone companies reputedly demonstrated. The end result was that instead of getting a new version of the DMS-100 switch out within six months, it was now taking eighteen months or longer, and the new version was of uncertain quality. This opened the door for AT&T and other rivals to grab sales away from Nortel. With their simpler software package containing fewer features and a modular format, they were able to get new versions out faster and with fewer flaws.

Compounding matters was a change in the way regional telephone carriers wanted to do business. Previously, they had purchased equipment every year through a number of small annual contracts. These annual contracts had usually been accompanied with price cuts in the order of 5 percent, which Nortel covered through annual cost-cutting drives. In 1992, however, the telephone carriers (notably, Ameritech) started to dangle big multiyear contracts in front of the equipment suppliers to gain pricing leverage. For example, for a five-year deal, they expected to get five years' worth of price cuts rolled into one. Nortel, sensing a do-or-die situation, had to bid substantially below its production costs in order to win contracts. This would require Nortel at some point to go through another round of major cost-cutting.

The problems encountered in the central office switch market in the early 1990s are also typical of a technology company facing a maturing product line. With its leading-edge products now widely adopted, sales were moderating. And rivals, having recouped from the initial shock of the disruptive technology, were fighting a renewed battle for market share. It is a dreaded situation for managers of technology companies, often a phase they fail to survive. Now Nortel was at this juncture, and Stern had to deal with it (perhaps if he were to write a second edition to his career book, he might add a warning to be wary of accepting an executive position in a technology company when its product cycle is in a late stage).

As a result of the problems in the core market of central office switches, Nortel's sales in North America showed poorly in the second quarter of 1992, contributing to earnings below expectations. This deterioration in financial performance kicked off a rather steep decline in share price over the second and third quarters of 1992. Investors in technology stocks are a skittish lot. Ever mindful that the competitive edge of a technology company could be erased overnight by a rival company leapfrogging ahead in product development, they tend to react in rather extreme fashion to any attenuation in earnings growth.

❦

In the spring of 1992, Stern attempted to have his hand-picked executive vice president, Edward Lucente, appointed as president, which would make him second-in-command after Stern in the CEO position. Lucente was a former IBM marketing ace who was expected to lead the charge into foreign markets. But the executives at BCE were becoming more concerned about the erosion of the core market for central office switches in North America. They wanted someone who would focus on the operations side, someone who would spearhead the revamping of the massive software program behind Nortel's digital switches.

In late September 1992, it was announced that BCE chairman Jean Monty would move over and become president and chief operating officer at Nortel, effective October 1. Unlike Scrivener who transferred from Bell to Nortel in the 1970s because the possibilities were more interesting, Monty was coming to sort things out. He would take over day-to-day operations, including responsibility for the three global product divisions and research. Monty would report to Stern, but being the point man for BCE, he would take the lead on guiding the research lab (already in crisis mode) through the necessary software upgrade and debugging of glitches.

Stern was aware of the need to fix the software before Monty was parachuted in, but he had delayed a full-fledged attack on the problem. As he later told a reporter, he "could never figure out how to do it without disrupting operations."[9] This admission comes the closest to confirming the claims of critics who declared that the success in boosting earnings during the Stern years had come about from a focus on the short term over the long term. In particular, in an effort to keep quarterly earnings marching ahead, spending on research and development was held back (resulting in a decline from 13 percent of total revenues in 1989 to 11 percent in 1992). As such, Nortel's spending on R&D was slipping back toward the industry average.

In the fourth quarter of 1992, there was a rebound in share prices. It was likely related to Monty's appointment and a strong third-quarter earnings report. Most of the financial improvement in that report came from growth in overseas markets and product lines such as PBX and data switches. The contribution to revenues from the core central office switching market in America was essentially flat.

In 1991, Nortel had nearly pulled even with AT&T in the US market for central office switching, grabbing an almost 40 percent share. But the following year, it slipped back to 35 percent, while AT&T's market share rose to 45 percent. Statistics like these brought further alarm. To be so close to surpassing their main rival, only to fall back, must have been disappointing. Despite the renewal of investor confidence, pressure was therefore still on to fix the software problem.

More good news came in January 1993 when a $270-million contract to supply digital switches to NTT was announced. The contract, part of the agreement signed in 1986, was for a bundle of DMS-10 switches. The new contract also extended the agreement to 1995, maintaining Nortel's bragging rights as the only foreign supplier in the Japanese market for central office switches.

Lending more support to the share price was the January release of fourth-quarter results showing record revenues and profits. Earnings in the quarter jumped 23 percent over the corresponding quarter the year before, coming at in $255.6 million. Per share earnings were $1.02, well ahead of the consensus estimate of $0.95 per share. Not surprisingly, share prices soared on the news. Analysts attributed the turn of events in part to Stern's reduction of operating expenses.

Within two days of the release of the positive fourth-quarter results, Stern shocked the business community by announcing his resignation as CEO, effective March 1, exactly four years after he took the position. On leaving a year before his contract was to expire, Stern joked, "I did not want to screw up my average,"[10] a reference to his tendency to stay about four years at each of the many corporations for which he had worked during his career.

He revealed his true feelings later on. His displeasure with the appointment of Monty over his choice of Lucente was evident when he told a reporter, "Nobody is going to shove a president down my throat."[11] There was also some tension between Stern and Monty. One of Monty's first actions was to present Stern with a proposal on how to fix the software problem. Stern agreed in principle, but disagreed over how fast and how much.

Overall, Stern felt his sojourn at Nortel had been a mistake. His feelings were summarized succinctly when he candidly stated, "… I got sucked into Northern."[12] During the week that news broke of his resignation, Stern gave a defense of his management approach, using the metaphor of the frog in a pot of water. He put it this way:

> If you turn up the heat slowly, the frog will get comfortable in the warm water and he will die when it starts to boil. But if the water's boiling and you toss in the frog, he'll jump right back out. I believe in dramatic change. It keeps you alert, alive. Incremental change doesn't succeed; the bureaucracy of the institution kills slow change. You've got to make the bold move. I really believe that.[13]

The problem with this approach, Stern went on to say, is that radical change scares people. It was probably his refusal to slow the pace of change, he added, that contributed to his image as a tyrant, an image he thought was inappropriately fueled by inaccurate reports in the press.

After passing the reigns over to Monty on March 1, Stern was looking forward to spending some time as a visiting professor at the Wharton School of the University of Pennsylvania, at which his son was enrolled. He was also planning to stay involved with Nortel in the capacity of chairman. "I will be carefully watching to see what this guy [Monty] does. I'm not disappearing,"[14] said Stern.

Shakespeare said that parting is such sweet sorrow, but in the case of Stern, it was likely more sweet than sorrowful, at least in monetary terms. He got a severance package worth more than $3 million (the estimated total value of two years of full salary and benefits), ten years added onto his pension plan, and the outstanding debt on his Maryland home paid off. It was a rather generous package, but it had all been agreed upon before Stern was hired, as part of the deal to lure him onto the team. According to this employment contract, Stern was to receive the severance deal in the event of his resignation or termination without cause.

Nor did Stern suffer monetarily during his last year of employment. He was paid, in addition to his regular salary of $916,666 and $249,038 in unused vacation leave, an incentive bonus of $975,000 based on the record corporate revenue and profit levels achieved for 1992. His total cash earnings in 1992 were $2.1 million. Then he received $3.3 million from options on Nortel shares.

About the same time, Edward Lucente, Stern's right-hand man, resigned. He too got a generous severance deal. He was paid a full year of salary and benefits, and had his $750,000 interest-free housing loan forgiven. Ordinary folk might be appalled by the generous severance packages that Lucente and Stern received, but such packages are not unusual at the executive level of major corporations in North America. Just like talented athletes earning millions in a season, talented executives need to be enticed onto a corporate team with attractive compensation.

⌗

The Stern era begins as a story about extending a competitive edge into new geographic market segments and of strict cost control administered by an outsider with a tough-guy reputation for implementing the hard choices that sometimes have to be taken. The early years were consequently ones of remarkable performance. Over 1990 and 1991—when the recession was dragging down the share prices of most other corporations—the price of Nortel shares marched straight up, more than doubling in value from the low established in early 1989. All told, over the four fiscal years from 1989 to 1992, Stern increased Nortel's revenues (with the assistance of several foreign acquisitions) by 56 percent to $8.4 billion and tripled net income to $536 million. It was quite an achievement to keep shareholder value and financial results going up during a recession.

Towards the end of the Stern years, with revenue growth coming to a standstill because of dependence on a maturing and increasingly competitive core market, the need for allocating resources to upgrading core market product lines was becoming obvious. And, beyond this defensive action, more resources would need to be allocated to developing new product lines in fast growing markets, if the growth pattern of the past was to be maintained.

But the increased allocation of resources to improve product lines presented a dilemma because it would mean diverting substantial revenues away from the bottom line, causing lower quarterly earnings. In the technology sector, missing earnings expectations by as little as a few cents per share can cut the stock price by more than half in virtually a day or two. This unwanted scenario may have been one reason why there was a delay in the actions required to upgrade and develop product lines. As such, Nortel in the early 1990s can be seen as an illustration of why technology firms sometimes get into trouble with the transition from old to new technologies.

Why Stern did what he did can only be a matter for conjecture. Perhaps he was not completely aware of the termites eating away at the foundation — so it was a matter of oversight. Then again, it could have been deliberate, a decision based on as simple a matter as the belief that performance in both the short term and long term could have been pulled off given enough time. Or it could have been a decision based on the rather complex matter of self-interest over corporate interest. Maintaining the track record in the short term would trigger millions of dollars in performance bonuses and stock options. Failure would not.

9

Monty and the Python

Fighting the Squeeze

When Jean Monty took over the chief executive position from Paul Stern, telecom-
munication analysts said Nortel was like an ocean liner listing
to one side. Monty's job would be to set the ship right and get
it steaming full speed ahead. Upon him would fall the weighty
responsibility of leading the turnaround of a multibillion-dollar corporation with a global workforce of over 55,000. A
daunting challenge to be sure, but if he failed, it would have
adverse consequences not only for his career, but also for the
thousands of employees and investors who depended upon
him. On the other hand, if he was successful, he would emerge
as a hero and would reap large financial rewards.

As it turned out, the Monty era at Nortel from 1993 to 1997
was a period of renewal and growth. As such, it is a superb case
study of a how a management team successfully dealt with a
crisis situation. How did the turnaround occur, and what did

Monty do to bring it about? How were employee morale improved, customers brought back to the fold, and the bottom line boosted?

Monty was forty-five years old when he accepted the chief executive position of Nortel. He was a physically imposing individual with a barrel chest and, although he was bald and bespectacled, he was charismatic. He had an aura of unflappable self-confidence that one reporter called Trudeauesque (referring to Canada's prime minister during the 1970s and early 1980s who was known for imperviousness in the face of pesky journalists). Another reporter labeled Monty's confidence a "force of nature."[1]

Monty left the chairman position at BCE to become the chief executive at Nortel in order to head off what BCE executives saw as a looming crisis at their subsidiary. Monty had joined BCE in 1974, where he had risen through the ranks and gained a reputation as a financial whiz. Before BCE, he had worked in the corporate finance department of investment dealer Merrill Lynch Canada Ltd. He was well educated, with a master's degree in economics from the University of Western Ontario and an MBA from the University of Chicago. Preparing him for the rigors of academe was the discipline of a Jesuit education during his adolescence in Montreal.

During his stay at Nortel, Monty was known as someone who did not hesitate to challenge those working for him. But he stopped short of the bullying tactics of which his predecessor was accused. One former coworker observed of Monty, "He's able to listen and change his mind, which is something not usual in those circles."[2] Another associate remarked, "During internal presentations, Monty is businesslike but friendly. With Stern, you knew he was always waiting to broadside you and show that he was smarter."[3] Where Stern was aloof, Monty built "rapport with people at all levels," said a third.[4]

When Jean Monty assumed the top job at Nortel, things initially were actually looking bright. The corporation had just won a huge contract to supply NTT with digital telephone switches, and record revenues and profits for the fourth quarter of 1992 had been announced. As a consequence, investor confidence was strong, and share values were close to previous highs. Within days of Monty's arrival, however, a discordant note emerged that would prove to be an early warning signal of the storms to come. On March 12, the vice president of corporate relations, John Strimas, revealed that a management review of global manufacturing operations was under way to find ways of improving cost effectiveness in the production of telephone switching equipment. "Increased competition...is forcing us to review our operations and [to] look for even more ways of cutting costs," Strimas said.[5]

The findings of the review were to be sent to senior management before June 30. Analysts speculated that the report would lead to a major restructuring of the corporation shortly afterward. Most likely to be affected would be the two largest plants—the switch manufacturing operations in Brampton, Ontario, and Raleigh, Northern Carolina—but smaller facilities, such as the ones in Texas and Malaysia, could also be affected. The warning signals became more distinct on March 25 when the corporation advised investors to expect first-quarter profits to come in below analysts' forecasts. The impending slip was attributed to increased spending on research and marketing campaigns, while revenues from the central office switch market remained flat.

The next day, Nortel shares plunged 11 percent on the stock exchange. Two investment firms downgraded their recommendations. Merrill Lynch lowered its rating to neutral, and Bunting Warburg rated Nortel a sell. Monty, however, portrayed a picture of optimism, saying that 1993 should still be a year of good performance despite the disappointing first quarter. One analyst agreed, pointing to strong fundamentals such as low debt and an ample backlog of orders.

When first-quarter financial results were released on April 27, profits were down 27 percent over the previous year, but the share price hardly budged as the market had already discounted the bad news. In the notes accompanying the first-quarter financial statements, the tone was still upbeat. The company was setting itself a new goal of raising its share of the global telecommunication equipment market from 7.5 percent to 12 percent, which would entail annual revenue growth of nearly 12 percent over the remainder of the decade. Mention was also made that spending on research and development would be a higher priority.

On May 8 came news that surely placed a greater urgency on the need to respond to mounting competitive threats. Nortel lost its status as the sole foreign supplier of switches to NTT when AT&T won a contract to supply eleven telephone switches to the Japanese telecommunication carrier. In doing so, AT&T beat out Nortel in the larger-sized class of telephone switches.

Meanwhile, other product lines and geographic markets were achieving breakthroughs, keeping pessimism at bay. FiberWorld, which hoped to repeat the amazing success of Digital World, looked like it could rise to the challenge when the lion's share of a five-year $650-million contract to install fiber-optic network equipment was awarded to Nortel by Pacific Bell. Also in May, a breakthrough in selling to the Chinese market appeared to be imminent when Zhu Rongji, the acting head of the Chinese government, visited Nortel's plant in Brampton on a trade mission and called for increased trade between China and Canada.

The actual breakthrough in China came the next month. On June 18, a memorandum of understanding, outlining an agreement wherein the corporation would set up manufacturing and research facilities in China in exchange for more telecommunication equipment sales, was signed between Nortel and the Chinese state planning commission. The details would be resolved through further discussion and negotiation. The opportunities for sales were truly immense. China's five-year plan called for the addition of 96 million lines to its telephone system, a job equivalent to building a telephone system four times the size of the entire Canadian one from scratch. Even more exciting was the potential beyond the immediate task described in the five-year plan: with only one telephone line for every 100 Chinese (compared to fifty-eight for every 100 persons in Canada), there was obviously much more work to be done.

In late June, however, the floodgates opened. On June 29, the corporation warned that it would post a loss in the second-quarter financial statements to be released in a few weeks time. Blame was laid on the continuing deterioration in the market for central office switching products, a deterioration related to aggressive price discounting and North American telephone companies trimming their capital expenditures. The news of Nortel's first quarterly loss in five years hit hard. Its market capitalization plummeted by nearly 25 percent in one day. Trading volume was heavy on all exchanges. About 2 million shares changed hands on each of the stock exchanges in Toronto and New York. Another 2.2 million traded on the smaller Montreal Stock Exchange — most of the trades, it was rumored, comprised block sales from the holdings of the Caisse de dépôt et placement du Québec, the giant pension fund in the province of Quebec.

Somewhat lost amid the calamitous market reaction was the announcement that Paul Stern would be leaving his last remaining station with the corporation. His replacement as chairman would be O. Bradford Butler, former chairman of consumer products giant Procter and Gamble, a move attesting to Nortel's desire to strengthen its focus on the customer. In addition, in another display of increased emphasis on the customer, the head of BNR would be replaced by a Bell Canada marketing executive, Brian Hewat.

Although the investment community had been warned to expect a loss when the second-quarter results were announced, they were not prepared for its magnitude. On July 22, Nortel reported a stunning loss of $1 billion for the three months to June 30. Much of the loss came from write downs and other special provisions, such as:

1. a charge of $282 million against earnings to close plants and lay off 5,200 employees (about 9 percent of the workforce)
2. an allocation of $158 million to a two-year project to upgrade the software of the DMS switches
3. a write down of $500 million of the goodwill associated with the acquisition of STC PLC

The $282-million charge to close plants and lay off people was the outcome of the earlier management review of manufacturing operations. The conclusion had been reached that radical restructuring was needed to get the break-even point of the corporation down low enough so that profits could be made in competition against AT&T. Previously, in the rush to meet exploding demand, the manufacturing apparatus had been thrown up in a rather hasty fashion; it was now time to rationalize these operations and to concentrate production in the more efficient plants.

The $158-million project to redesign the DMS switch software would aid in the struggle against AT&T by improving the quality and customer appeal of the software. That the massive program—24 million lines of code—was in need of fixing was obvious. It had strayed from the design principles set out by Cashin and Beaumont back in the late 1970s and now required inordinate amounts of time to incorporate new features. And adding new code at times adversely interacted with other parts of the program, precipitating system-wide failures. The redesign strategy would therefore focus on segmenting the program into self-contained modules, which would reduce the interactions and thereby speed up the process of adding and testing new features.

The $500-million write down of goodwill connected with the purchase of STC PLC, nearly a third of the total, was taken because, according to Monty, the acquisition had not lived up to expectations. Synergies between the Canadian and British transmission facilities did not materialize to the extent anticipated. Nor did it help that the British pound went through a major devaluation in the early 1990s.

At the same time the $1-billion loss was announced, Monty revealed that the submarine cable operations of STC PLC were to be sold to Alcatel Cable SA for $900 million, an amount that would cancel the remaining STC goodwill on the books (once the transaction was completed in early 1994). The STC operations were doing well but were not at the top of their market niche, so Nortel wanted to redirect these resources to markets where they could be a dominant supplier.

An interesting aspect of the sale was the time and place of the news release—Mississauga at 3:00 AM. This odd hour was dictated by stock market regulations that required announcements relating to international acquisitions be made in such a way that investors in one country were not favored over those in another. With Nortel stock trading in London, New York,

Toronto, and Tokyo (and the transaction having implications for the Paris bourse because of the French purchaser), meeting this requirement was quite a challenge. After a bit of research, it was discovered that 3:00 AM EST was the only time stock markets in all affected countries were closed: it was 8:00 AM in London, 9:00 AM in Paris, and 4:00 PM in Tokyo.

After the avalanche of bad news so early in his tenure, some observers were prompted to compare the first year of Monty's leadership to the period when an elected politician takes hold of the reigns of power and uses the transition phase to administer stiff medicine that is blamed on a predecessor. Monty himself threw cold water on such suggestions. He said Stern's departure just happened to coincide with the need to face up to the maturing of the core market for digital switches. But analysts at the time could not help speculating otherwise. As one of them said, "There is a natural predisposition to lay all the blame on an outgoing CEO, a tendency to sweep several problems into a tidy portfolio and dispose of it."[6]

After the announcement of the $1-billion loss in the summer of 1993, Monty set about reorganizing the corporation, creating a management structure split into two operating groups. Nortel World Trade, under the direction of James Long, would pursue marketing and business activities by geographic region. Nortel North America, under the direction of John Roth, would serve the customer base in North America and guide global product development. Nortel North America would be subdivided into four product groupings:

1. public carrier networks (serving transmission and switching needs of telephone companies)

2. broadband networks (serving transmission and switching needs of cable TV and long-distance carriers)

3. enterprise networks (servicing the internal communication needs of corporations and government departments)

4. wireless networks (serving the infrastructure requirements of mobile telephone providers)

Over the next two years, Monty visited eighteen of the company's main locations twice, participating in town-hall meetings, breakfasts with rising stars, and other activities aimed at communicating and boosting morale. He often held question-and-answer sessions with no managers present so that he could get feedback directly from the grassroots. Videos and brochures about the transition were produced and distributed. All senior executives were sent on the road to meet employees. Through this process of education and communication, Monty hoped to build rapport and support for the changes going on in the corporation. He was a firm believer in such communication: "You can never overcommunicate to your own employees about what you are doing—both for them to understand and to be able to communicate to your customers."[7]

Another area that Monty stressed was the improvement of customer relations. "Empathy for customers is so bloody important in any business," he declared.[8] He felt customer satisfaction was so crucial that he hired the Gallup Organization to carry out quarterly surveys of customer satisfaction and tied senior management bonuses to the results. Research and development had to be better tailored to needs in the marketplace; to this end, the function was to be distributed more geographically and put in closer contact with customer requirements in particular markets. The Nortel spirit was to be one of looking outward, a can-do attitude of finding ways to create something new and useful for clients. Navel gazing and internecine machinations were certainly to be avoided.

⌘

The loneliness of the long-distance runner is nothing in comparison to the loneliness of the turnaround artist. Looking back on his stay at Nortel a few years afterward, Monty recounted how stressful it was to assume control and begin the turnaround. In his own words: "It was a little overwhelming. The first six months were rough. Sometimes you are all alone. Six months in the life of a corporation is not a very long time, but when you're in it, you think it's an eternity. You just close your eyes and go forward."[9] Despite the perils of his mixed metaphor, Monty's first six months at the helm would prove to be a major turning point for the corporation, a watershed that laid the basis for renewal as one of the leading beacons in the telecommunication industry.

His early days of trial and tribulation were not made any easier by some members of the Canadian press who persisted in raising social issues relating to the rumored plant closures and job loses. Monty had little patience for this line of inquiry, viewing it as simpleminded. At a press conference after the 1992 annual meeting, he testily responded to one reporter's inquiries about the social impact of layoffs with the statement: "We're talking about having…large international corporations with 200,000 employees with greater economies of scale going after us, competing on price, and [you're] talking about 200 jobs moving back and forth between two plants."[10]

On September 1, 1993, Nortel announced that two Canadian plants—one in London, Ontario, and another in Amherst, Nova Scotia—would be closed as part of a first round of the restructuring measures announced earlier. The London plant closure came as a shock to officials in the Canadian Auto Workers (CAW) union. It would suffer a membership decline of 600, bringing the cumulative reduction in CAW's Nortel membership to nearly half over the past two years. Not surprisingly, the union called on the Canadian federal government to investigate. As one CAW director said, "It's unbelievable that the federal government will allow this to happen. Ottawa should require the company to justify the closure."[11]

The timing of the closure was not ideal. The CAW labor contract would be expiring in February, just months away. With union executives inflamed, negotiations would be tough and prickly. At a press conference in December, the first salvo was fired when the union secretary-treasurer warned that a strike was likely if the London shutdown was not called off. Taking a hard line, Nortel's response was that the closure was not negotiable; their priority was to contain and reduce costs.

Around this time, Monty broadened the restructuring and cost-cutting program to include management at all levels. In a letter to 3,000 managers and executives, Monty declared that employees could not be expected to embrace tough measures unless their superiors led by example. He was therefore instituting a freeze on all pay raises for managerial staff in 1994. In addition, corporate limousines and chauffeurs were to be eliminated. As well, the aviation department would be dismantled and its four corporate jets sold off.

Cynics might have said the sacrifices at the managerial levels were just window dressing for the contract negotiations with its largest union, but others saw it as a more fundamental effort to win broader support within the organization for the coming changes and sacrifices. Stern's open enjoyment of corporate limousines, jets, and other executive perks during an earlier period of austerity may have been a factor contributing to his problems with poor morale and resistance within the ranks. Monty's austerity moves at the senior ranks would remove at least this impediment.

In the midst of the negotiations, fourth-quarter and annual results were released. The overall result for 1993 was a $878-million loss, the largest ever. If the $940 million in special provisions taken in 1993 were excluded, Nortel would have an operating profit of $62 million, still way down from the record profit of the year before. Part of the blame for the predicament was the millions of dollars required to revamp the software for its mainstay DMS switches and develop new products in the areas of wireless communication and broadband networks.

The contract negotiations with CAW went right down to the wire. At virtually the last minute before the deadline of midnight on February 25, a strike was averted. The union was hoping to head off the impending plant closure by securing a deal similar to the job-security agreements reached with the automobile companies the year earlier. Those aspirations were, however, put aside in return for improved pensions, a cost of living allowance, and annual pay raises between 1 and 1.5 percent over the length of the three-year pact.

After the furor surrounding the London plant closing in 1993, implementation of the remaining phases of the cutback plan were some time in coming. It was not until over a year later, in the first half of 1995, that the ax began to really swing again, and it was announced that 1,200 jobs would be eliminated at Nortel's flagship plant in Bramalea, Ontario. The union reaction was vociferous. Buzz Hargrove, president of the CAW, angrily denounced the move, saying, "It is part of a deliberate strategy to move their manufacturing out of Canada and to low-wage countries."[12] Jean Monty challenged the claim. He said: "It makes for good rhetoric, but we have no strategy to exit Canada."[13] The number of manufacturing jobs in Canada, he added, had increased from 9,200 to 10,500 over the previous five years, and the bulk of the company's research and development jobs still remained in Canada.

A few days later, the CAW president followed up his criticisms with a more substantial attack in a letter to *The Globe and Mail*, one of Canada's leading national newspapers. Marshaling statistics from his research department, the main contention of the union leader was that Nortel was violating its contract with Canadian citizens. According to Hargrove, Nortel had been the recipient of government research and development tax credits totaling at least $880 million over the years, the objective of which was supposedly to stimulate Canadian production and exports. Yet Nortel had chopped 3,000 jobs (or 25 percent of its Canadian workforce) in the two years since 1993, while simultaneously opening state-of-the-art production facilities in Mexico and China.

This picture did not make sense to CAW executives. Nortel was having its cake and eating it too, reputedly enjoying the benefits of subsidies but bearing few of the social obligations. According to union estimates, the company had received at least $100,000 in research and development subsidies for every manufacturing job left over after the latest round of layoffs. This was not good value in their opinion; to correct the situation, the federal government should start attaching strings to the handouts. A principal objective of those conditions would, of course, be to keep jobs in Canada.

Corporate officials responded that Nortel was a multinational corporation that had to deal with the forces of global business environments. To continue making a product in-house when it could be purchased more cheaply from a foreign supplier was a recipe for corporate failure, they added. Competitors will obtain better efficiencies and put the higher-cost operation out of business. They concluded with the point that setting up factories and jobs in other countries was the price of admission to those markets. It was required in order to generate sales abroad.

As it turned out, there was no need to tie employment levels to government credits for research and development. Within a year or so, growth at Nortel pushed employment back up again in the Canadian operations, eventually to levels higher than before. Highlights of job growth included the 5,000 hired in 1997 to work at BNR and the 1,000 hired the same year for plants in Montreal to make transmission products.

At about the same time as the CAW was campaigning against the Bramalea closure, institutional shareholders were getting hot under the collar too. It was an unusual step for the buttoned-down group of portfolio managers to air their grievances in the press. Normally, such matters are resolved behind closed doors. Needless to say, under attack from both fronts—labor and capital—Jean Monty may have felt somewhat lonely and beleaguered. One or the other side may be disgruntled at any given time, but both simultaneously was quite an achievement. It was perhaps a measure of the difficult situation from which Monty was trying to extricate his corporation.

Several pension funds, including the Caisse de dépôt et placement du Québec, Ontario Municipal Employees Retirement System, and Ontario Teachers Pension Plan Board, had released a statement criticizing management's proposal to expand the stock-option plan. The changes would increase the number of stock options to 40 million from 25 million. If all those options were exercised, they would increase the total number of outstanding shares by 16 percent. This would be too much dilution of the equity base, an increase in the number of shares that could materially lower shareholder value. A more reasonable dilution, said the pension funds, would be 5 percent of shares outstanding, the norm for companies the size of Nortel.

The rationale for the expansion in the number of options was that it was needed to attract and retain top managerial and technical talent. The alternative would be to lose the talented staff to US firms dangling more lucrative options packages. BCE, then owner of 52 percent of the shares, was in favor of the amended option plan, so it looked like the proposal would easily sail though the voting at the annual meeting weeks away. As it turned out, a slightly watered-down version did pass. As in the case of the disgruntled unions, the worries over dilution proved groundless; within a year or so, Nortel shares were rising on their way to levels even higher than before.

Over the 1980s, the North American public telephone system had metamorphosed into a tremendously intricate computer network in which telephone sets functioned as terminals and the central office switches functioned as processors performing the functions of directing message traffic and supporting call-control services (e.g., call forwarding and call identification). Nortel had started out selling both the hardware and software components, but now that all the hardware infrastructure was just about in place, it was becoming more like a software company, earning its revenues from software design, upgrades, and add-ons. And like most software outfits, the margins on sales were very lucrative.

One big problem confronting Nortel in the early 1990s, however, was that it was not well-positioned to provide software enhancements in a timely and error-free fashion. As the size of the program mushroomed, the time to get new versions to market lengthened from a few months to over a year. In addition, a change made in one part of the code could adversely interact with parts of the code elsewhere, complicating the testing process and increasing the odds that a glitch would get through.

This in itself was undesirable, but making it more so was the fact that AT&T's equipment subsidiary had gotten ahead of Nortel in setting up a better procedure for software enhancements. Developed by their research arm, Bell Labs, the Advanced Intelligent Network (AIN) separated the call-control software from the switching software and put it into a more powerful computer outside the switching apparatus. As such, it would be much easier and quicker to improve and expand the number of call-control tasks telephone users could perform when using their telephone sets.

In setting aside a reserve of $158 million for a two-year redesign project, Monty accelerated the efforts already in place to "find a cure for the common code,"[14] or more specifically, to refashion the massive 24-million-line software program more along the lines of the modular and AIN format of its main rival—and then some. The new software, called Generic Services Frame, had four different modules:

1. Base (provides the basic operating system for all switches)
2. Telecom (provides signal processing standards)
3. Product (differentiates switches, e.g., DMS-100 vs. DMS-300)
4. Customer (customer control-call features)

The new architecture was implemented in stages, more or less on schedule and budget. Once in place, the redesign reduced time to market by 50 to 75 percent, doubled the productivity of designers, and reduced design defects by a ratio of four to one. With this more efficient process in place, new software features could be introduced in several waves during the year.

After several years of flat or slightly declining revenues, the central office product line began to experience growth toward the end of Monty's term despite the predictions of most analysts. They had thought the central office switching market was mature. But their forecasts were off the mark. During Monty's term, revenues in the core product group were up 5 percent in 1994, 8 percent in 1995, and 7 percent in 1996. This was slow growth but still "better than many had thought possible."[15] One reason for the above-expectations growth was the software upgrades; another was the requirement to upgrade telephone networks in order to cope with the advent of the Internet.

⚛

The $1-billion loss in the second quarter of 1993 knocked Nortel's share price down several more notches in the days following the news release. With this latest buffeting, the share price was more than 50 percent below the high reached earlier in the year. In total, at least $7.5 billion had been erased from market capitalization. The magnitude of the decline can be illustrated through a comparison with upstart switch maker Newbridge Networks. The total value on the stock exchange of the latter corporation was now almost two-thirds of Nortel's, even though Newbridge's annual sales were just 4 percent of its larger rival.

Several credit rating agencies put Nortel on ratings watch after the big loss was announced. Within two weeks, two of them had followed up with downgrades. First came Dominion Bond Rating Service Ltd. and then Standard and Poors Corp. The latter lowered its rating on senior debt from single-A plus to single-A. The reason for the downgrade given by Standard and Poors was that, in its opinion, profitability and cash flow would remain under pressure due to continued intense price competition and the undertaking of a major software development for affected products.

Yet in the midst of the gloom, there were glimmers of hope. "My first reaction to this story is, 'Let's buy Nortel stock,'" said Canadian telecommunication analyst Ian Angus.[16] His sentiments were echoed by a few other experts, contrasting with the thumbs-down sentiment in the stock market. The experts knew Nortel had been down before, but that it had always come back. Its renewed commitment to research and development and the opportunities to penetrate foreign markets were still big pluses. Investors now had a chance to buy into a good company at a steep discount.

Under Monty, Nortel was to overcome its troubles and experience a renewal that returned the company to its previous status as a premier growth company. Investors who had heeded the call of analyst Angus to invest in Nortel at the nadir of its woes in 1993 would have seen the value of their shares more than quadruple over the years Monty was at the helm. In 1993, Nortel was seen as a technology company dependent upon a declining core product line facing increased competition from a bigger rival, as well as lagging in developing new products for fast-growing markets like wireless and ATM systems. Thus, prospects for Nortel did not look promising at the time.

Yet, the doubters were proved wrong. Monty found a way to navigate through a succession of perils such as labor strife and investor disenchantment. And with his expertise in financial matters and his political acumen, he successfully dealt with the DMS software problems while financing expansion into new geographical markets and expansion of research and development. Then, of course, there was the initiative and skills of his lieutenant, John Roth, who assembled a line of wireless equipment products that picked up the slack for the core product line of central office switches.

Like leaders in the political realm who often end up in the good books of posterity, Monty, the business leader, had a little help from the external environment. It cooperated in generating a favorable groundswell of demand for telecommunication equipment. The auctioning off of government licenses to operate new wireless devices, as well as the pervasive deregulation of telecommunication sectors around the globe, fueled equipment demand by increasing the number of players in the carrier services industry. However, that Monty and his right-hand man, Roth, caught and rode these tailwinds was to their credit.

After the restructuring plan was announced in the summer of 1993, the price of Nortel shares began to recover. As revenues and earnings came in at, or above, expectations in quarters over the rest of 1993 and throughout 1994, value investors nibbling at the stock were joined by investors seeking to ride turnaround situations. By the end of 1994, the share price was up more than 50 percent from its low in 1993.

When the financial results for 1994 were released, they reinforced the sentiment that Nortel was back on track. Earnings rebounded to $404 million or $1.60 per share. Asset sales had inflated earnings by $0.40 per share, but analysts were still happy as the results were slightly above their forecast. Particularly encouraging, however, was a 9 percent increase in revenues to a record level of $8.9 billion, originating mainly from growth in Latin American and Chinese markets. Monty's focus on expanding into overseas markets had been a key element.

Monty was most pleased with the sales growth, which ended a three-year period of flatness. "This is the element I am most pleased with. It shows we are really making progress with our customers on our product portfolio," he said.[17] And looking forward, prospects were good for more of the same, considering that the order backlog jumped 16 percent in the fourth quarter of 1993. That would be good news for earnings growth too since more revenues would be flowing directly to the bottom line because costs were on a downward path as a result of the cost-cutting program.

The price of Nortel shares continued to rise in the first quarter of 1995, but this rally was erased in the second and third quarters. The retreat started with the announcement in late April of a drop in profits for the first quarter compared to the same quarter the year before. However, the impression of declining profits was misleading due to the fact that the earnings of the base quarter were inflated by the proceeds from the sale of a plant in Saskatoon. Excluding this earlier one-time gain, earnings would have actually shown an increase of 300 percent over the same quarter the year before. But the market overlooked this statistical distortion. Or perhaps it was worried about other things.

One of them, as mentioned, could have been the potentially dilutive impact of management's plan to increase the number of grants under the employee stock-option plan. Institutional shareholders took the unusual step of airing their grievances publicly on this matter, so it is a reasonable conjecture that this fear led them to lighten up on their stock holdings over the ensuing months. Another worry was created when AT&T announced in the third quarter that it was going to split itself into three separate publicly traded companies. One of the new companies, called Lucent Technologies Inc, would comprise the equipment manufacturing operations of AT&T. Unleashed from its parent, the manufacturing operations would be a more formidable rival.

The slide in 1995 was halted with the release in late October of the third-quarter financial statements. Profits rose 42 percent to $81 million, while revenues jumped 24 percent to $2.5 billion. The order backlog shot up nearly 50 percent to $2.7 billion, a very bullish sign going forward. Sales and orders were fueled by gains in new product segments such as wireless equipment and in new markets including China.

Monty said the higher-than-expected revenue gain allowed the company to finance additional research and development; expenses for this function in the first nine months in 1995 were $1.1 billion, almost 16 percent of revenues. The increase went into new products in the wireless and broadband transmission markets. The extra revenues could have gone to swelling profits even more, but Monty's eye was more on the long term.

When the financial performance for 1995 was announced in early 1996, the price of Nortel shares had snapped back. Aiding the drive upward was a growing feeling that Nortel was on the verge of winning a huge $1-billion contract to supply wireless equipment to Sprint Corp. It was a sign that Nortel had emerged as a serious contender in the market for wireless equipment against the likes of entrenched players Motorola and Ericsson.

The 1995 Annual Report further contributed to the image of a company staging a strong recovery. That year, Nortel achieved net income of $478 million, or $1.85 per share, on revenues of $10.7 billion. The increase in profit was slightly better than expectations. The 20 percent growth in annual revenues was another cause for celebration, and analysts applauded the financial improvements.

Over 1996, quarterly releases of financial results continued to impress. Profits jumped 33 percent in the first quarter and 40 percent in the third quarter, exceeding the average forecast of the analysts. Sales growth in the wireless and enterprise systems product lines was complemented unexpectedly by growth in the product lines of central office switches and transmission equipment. They were coming on stronger because of unforeseen demand placed on the public telephone system by the rise of the Internet. This new medium was inducing telephone carriers to upgrade their installed DMS switches in order to provide second telephones lines into homes and ISDN capability for greater capacity in handling Internet communication. Demand was also on the rise for the high-speed fiber-optic transmission systems into which Nortel had poured so much research and development effort.

Another factor in the increase in earnings over 1996 was a winding down of spending on research and development following the ramp-up in Monty's early years. Management now wanted to let research and development return to more normal levels and let the fruits of their efforts show up more in the bottom line. With enhanced momentum in earnings, more brokerage analysts were taking notice, usually recommending Nortel as a buy.

Toward the end of 1996, the number of analysts in the United States and Canada who were covering the company had risen to an unprecedented forty-three. A September investment meeting arranged by Nortel attracted record numbers. This mounting enthusiasm within the investment community consequently led to an increased valuation for Nortel shares, as indicated by an expansion in the price-to-earnings ratio to a level above the historical average. This, along with growth in earnings per share, was a factor behind an appreciation of more than 50 percent in Nortel share price over 1996.

That year closed with Nortel racking up a 32 percent profit gain to $623 million on revenues of $12.8 billion. That meant earnings per share of $2.40 easily surpassed the $2.17 per share record achieved in 1992. According to an analyst from Yorkton Securities, the company had succeeded "in pushing its growth beyond the industry average through its foreign expansion and product development."[18] Overseas markets were now accounting for almost 40 percent of total revenues. Not to be overlooked was the impact of a lower cost structure achieved through the restructuring plan announced in 1993.

A laudable aspect of the reemergence of Nortel as a growth story was that it was done without sacrificing the balance sheet. In fact, the balance sheet was actually strengthened as the proportion of total debt to total capitalization declined over Monty's term from 44 percent to 25 percent. Debt was thus relatively unimportant in financing acquisitions, development of new products, marketing efforts, and other strategies underlying the turnaround. More important sources of funds were internal cash flow and asset sales totaling $2 billion. The asset sales not only raised funds but got the company out of product lines, such as submarine cable, in which profit margins were low or there was no hope of becoming a dominant supplier.

A vital ingredient in the success of Nortel during the Monty period was spending on research and development. It rose as high as 16 percent of total revenues before sliding back down to 14 percent, still one of the highest rates of research expenditure in the telecommunication industry. That level represented well over $1 billion in spending per year.

The high levels of spending on research were partly a reflection of the numerous opportunities to cater to the rapidly evolving needs of telecommunication service providers. In generating a constant flow of new and improved products, the research and development function allowed Nortel to diversify its product portfolio into fast-growing niches so that its growth remained vigorous as the core product line matured. It is not an easy feat to pull off—many technology companies never recover the growth pattern that their first core product line gave them.

And it was just not sheer magnitude in spending that won the day. The research and development process was made smarter by tying it more closely to what customers wanted. Rather than having a group of engineers and programmers design products with the greatest number of "oh wow" technical features, the objective increasingly became to first consult with the customers and find out what they needed so that research and development could be tailored to that.

Helping in this process would be the decentralization of research and development, a distribution of staff and equipment to be in closer contact with customers. Also helping in focusing on the needs of the customer were the opinion surveys monitoring customer satisfaction. Such was the upheaval in the requirements of customers that in the mid-1990s, nearly half of Nortel's marketable products were less than five years old.

As Monty's term at Nortel came to an end in the fall of 1997, the price of Nortel shares was standing approximately four times as high as the low reached in the summer of 1993. The rise in his final year was fueled by further positive momentum in sales and profits. First-quarter earnings were up 33 percent to a record level of $112 million, boosted by wireless and business enterprise lines. Second-quarter profit soared ahead of analysts' expectations, rising 56 percent to $169 million. Third-quarter earnings leapt 40 percent. In October, Nortel's board of directors approved a two-for-one split of the company's common shares, effective in 1998, increasing the number of outstanding shares to 520 million. Among those shareholders pleased with ongoing appreciation in Nortel shares was Monty himself: his $2-million compensation in 1996 was nicely augmented by $4.3 million (Canadian) from exercising stock options.

⌗

In 1993, Nortel was in a crisis situation—the python was coiled menacingly close by. The company's core product line was in a mature market capable of providing no better than flat growth rates. Even worse, AT&T had strengthened its products and was taking away business. With its main market slowing down and under attack by a larger rival, the company's future looked uncertain, to say the least.

Facing up to the crisis, Monty had devised a multifaceted rescue plan. One main prong was to shore up the home base and retain existing clientele in its core market through a restructuring and cost-cutting initiative that would bring down manufacturing costs and improve the timeliness and quality of its DMS switches. The other major prong involved getting out of low-growth niches and redirecting resources to high-growth markets, especially those in which the company could be expected to rank in the top three. This strategy produced growth in sales to offset the slowdown in its mainstay line, thus maintaining the overall growth trajectory of the past.

Repositioning into faster and more promising product markets required changes in several areas. One was increased allocation of resources to the research and development function in order to develop and enhance product lines. Another was an internal reorganization into two operating groups and subdividing one of them by product line. This latter subdivision would be particularly important for improving the structure of incentives, giving responsibility for individual business lines to one manager. Each product line would, in effect, be run as if it were an enterprise of its own, with formerly centralized functions such as research and development distributed (at least in part) down to the product line.

Another main feature of the rescue plan was a renewed focus on the customer. It was thought that Nortel had lost its sensitivity to the needs of its clients. Customers liked Nortel's switches because they could provide the most valued-added services of any on the market, but they were increasingly complaining about delays in receiving upgrades and addressing software bugs. Nortel had to be outwardly focused, mindful of the challenges that had to be surmounted. Without this leadership in directing attention to external targets, a corporation could easily lapse into an unproductive focus on internal disagreements and battles.

From 1993 to 1997, Nortel went from $8.1 billion to $15.4 billion in sales, an increase of 90 percent. Growth in earnings per share over his term averaged close to 25 percent per year. Accolades consequently poured in. Monty was named Canadian CEO of the Year in 1997. More importantly, Lynton Wilson, the head of BCE, was happy. His comments as Monty's term came to an end were: "He's an outstanding field commander who inspires his troops with strong leadership. What Jean was able to do early on was focus on the key issues: customer satisfaction, employee morale, and technology."[19]

In addition to professional success, Monty enjoyed personal success. Following his term at Nortel, he was promoted to his boss's job, the chief executive position at BCE.

10

Roth's
Wireless Feat

On a crisp, sunny Saturday morning in the fall of 1997, John Roth was leaning against his red 1967 Corvette parked in the winding driveway of his treed estate an hour north of Toronto. A streak of grease on his hands revealed that earlier he was tinkering under the hood. Wearing a sweater, Roth was relaxed and affable as he talked to a reporter about his earlier cars—in particular, one unreliable MG convertible he had to virtually rebuild from new parts. That Roth loved fast cars was obvious. Every now and then, whenever time permitted, he would hop into the Corvette (with plates BIG VET) or one of his other vintage sports cars for a quick spin around the grounds. His everyday car, the one used for traveling to work, was a Porsche 911 Turbo.

A few months earlier, Roth, attired in a business suit, was sitting next to Jean Monty in a Nortel boardroom. The two were being interviewed following the announcement that Roth would succeed Monty as chief executive. According to the reporter, Monty was "relaxing like a reigning monarch in a fuchsia-colored chair," while Roth was "stiff and uncomfortable, his lanky frame at war with his perch."[1] He seemed to be awkward talking about his promotion. Fast cars and the rapidly evolving telecommunication sector are what he likes to talk about more.

While Roth's body language was at odds with the honor bestowed upon him, Monty's explanation for appointing Roth was not. He said that Roth was selected because of "the breadth of his capabilities...his knowledge of the business, his capability to deliver results...[and] his ability to communicate with employees and customers."[2]

The son of an airline radio operator, Roth was born in Lethbridge, Alberta, but his teenage years were spent in Pointe-Claire, outside of Montreal. As a young man, he studied electrical engineering at McGill University in Montreal, graduating with a master's degree in 1966. The long hair and bell-bottom trousers of the counterculture era in the 1960s had no attraction for him. Upon graduation, he set out straightaway to find work as a design engineer.

To land his first job, he attended a McGill job fair. A recruiter for Nortel was present, and Roth approached him with application in hand. But the future chief executive was turned down. The recruiter told him that Nortel wanted engineers with management potential. Instead, Roth found his first job at RCA Canada Ltd., designing antennas in their (now defunct) satellite division.

He worked there for three years until, dissatisfied with the way senior managers were treating employees, he left to join Nortel's satellite research division, which was instrumental in the pioneering ANIK satellites (that division also has since disappeared.) When BNR was set up as a subsidiary of Nortel, Roth transferred over with other research staff. He worked there as a design engineer until 1974, after which he was promoted to the management ranks at Nortel. Next, he moved through various project management and marketing positions to become the general manager of the station apparatus division in 1977. He was just thirty-five years old, the youngest person ever to reach the general manager level at Nortel.

His climb up the corporate ladder sped ahead like one of his sports cars. The next year, he was promoted to vice president of manufacturing operations and, in 1982, he was appointed to president of BNR. Again, he set the record for being the youngest to reach the vice president and president levels within the company. He stayed at BNR until he was assigned to headquarters as vice president of product line management in 1986.

As he moved up the ranks, Roth increasingly gained a reputation as someone who always accomplished his assignments with flying colors. He was known as a low-key type of guy, possessing little of the arrogance characteristic of many in the mold of a rising corporate star. As a manager, he avoided bullying tactics when dealing with subordinates, preferring a gentle hand. His approach was to give people room to grow and make them feel valued. In his view, the best way to motivate employees was to give them a vision. Effective leaders were those who could paint pictures that captured the imagination of their staff. As he once said: "If you can show people a compelling image, they'll work harder than you could ever order them to work."[3]

Whatever area Roth was assigned to, he quickly mastered the details of the field and won respect as a manager who knew his stuff. At the same time, he did not get lost in minutiae or bogged down in processes. He had a knack for the "fifty-foot view," for strategic thinking, spotting trends, and seizing growth opportunities. In other words, he had an orientation for detecting and capitalizing on discontinuities. As he stated:

We're in an industry of huge opportunity, and the task is to see the opportunity. I guess I've had a knack for seeing opportunity. Where other people see problems, I see opportunities. There are problems, obviously, but...you know, those are just the things in the way of the opportunity.[4]

But he had more than a demonstrated ability to spot opportunities in markets and technologies. Part of his career was doing system design, which required assessing technological trends in order to produce designs that would last. That experience gave him an eye for spotting where the leverage would be in a technological system—that is, he was good at identifying those parts that would control the value. Those parts tended to be the complex elements that other companies had problems making, and they were evolving according to Moore's Law. Developing a new product, Roth stated, is not "...designing it for today, it's designing it through several cycles of technology...and as technology evolves, these components get cheaper, these components get more powerful, the whole design becomes better...as opposed to it becoming obsolete."[5]

Another thing to which Roth attributed his success was careful selection of the projects on which he focused his efforts. Success was tied to not just doing a good job, but doing so in the right place and time. In his words:

I never worked on something that I didn't believe would be successful. There were projects at times I was given [that led me to say] "This project's not going to go anywhere," and I'd kill it. I would say, "It'd be a waste of energy, waste of my time, waste of the time of the rest of the organization." So I'd kill things....If something's going to fail, it's better we cancel it early than cancel it late.[6]

Probably the best demonstration of his abilities, the one that led directly to his promotion to the chief executive position, was his initiation and development of the wireless product line. While in charge of product-line management in the late 1980s, he led a campaign to take Nortel into wireless telephone communication. Senior executives at the time were focused on beefing up the company's core competency in central office digital switches, and they did not want to dilute their concentration or resources in pursuit of uncertain chances in a field dominated by entrenched suppliers such as Motorola and Ericsson. Roth nevertheless continued to press the argument that use of mobile telephones would soar and lift demand for switches used in wireless networks—especially high-end versions such as Nortel's.

After getting the green light from chief executive Paul Stern in 1991, a new division, called the Wireless Systems Group, was established under Roth as president. And as he went about setting up the product line, it became obvious that he was right about demand for wireless digital switches taking off. The upsurge in orders subsequently made the most important contribution to Nortel's financial turnaround in the mid-1990s. His group of wireless products rose from almost zero to 23 percent of company sales over the 1990s. It was Roth's foray into wireless products that largely renewed Nortel's growth trajectory after the core product line of central office switches slowed down in the early 1990s.

Before becoming chief executive in 1997, there were other stops on the corporate ladder. In early 1994, he was handed the presidency of a new division—Nortel North America—and not long after, the chief operating officer position. In the latter role, he engineered a streamlining of the organization to reduce internal bureaucracy and strengthen focus on customers. In the process, the dissension stemming from the cost-cutting Stern era was redirected toward a focus on the external environment. By the time the fifty-five-year-old Roth assumed the top job in the fall of 1997, the morale problem had largely vanished.

Those who have worked for him typically remark that he was an accessible manager who liked to roam around and talk to people. Communication has always been important to him. As he became more prominent within Nortel, he proved equally accessible to the media. His answers during interviews were candid. A couple of months into the chief executive position, a reporter asked him to explain what caused the crisis at Nortel back in 1993. Roth's response was: "In the 1980s, we fell into the trap of paying too much attention to the products we had, and we ignored new products and new customers."[7] He still bristles, it is said, at how Nortel almost missed getting into wireless communications back in the early 1990s.

Just after the announcement of his appointment to the chief executive position, Roth was asked by another reporter what he intended to do as the top person at Nortel. "My strategy," replied Roth, "is to be in every high-growth area of telecommunication."[8] Thus, Roth was not afraid to move away from the security of a core competency. In the topsy-turvy world of technology, corporations need to anticipate trends, be prepared to turn on a dime, and jump into surging markets.

Roth would surely chuckle when he thought back to the McGill job fair he attended in the 1960s, when the recruiter from Nortel said they needed engineers who could be managers. At the time, he just wanted to be a designer, so he said no thanks. As CEO of Nortel, Roth's priorities were now different. "Well, I used to design products. Now, I design businesses,"[9] he said. And he might have added that his company

was now perhaps like one of the sports cars in his collection—
a carefully restored machine purring out a lot of power.

In the early 1990s, Nortel's hopes for a repeat of the Digital
World success were not pinned on the embryonic wireless division (that was reserved for FiberWorld). Indeed, the entry into
wireless was late and unpromising. Cellular phones had been
out for some time, and the market was dominated by big companies such as Motorola and Ericsson. But Roth had foreseen an
opportunity to make up for lost time. A discontinuity was arising that played to Nortel's forte.

Rapid growth in mobile telephone usage was taxing the call-
handling capacity of analog cellular networks, creating a bot-
tleneck that would be relieved only by shifting toward digital
service, or Personal Communication Service (PCS) networks.
Whereas existing cellular service involved transmitting handset
radio signals to widely spaced cell receiver stations, digital networks involved transmitting radio signals to more closely
spaced and lower-power base stations. The latter were so small
that they could be tucked away in parking lots, on the sides of
buildings, or at traffic intersections.

Digital networks would not only expand call-processing
capacity, but introduce new benefits to consumers. Handsets
would be smaller and more lightweight because they did not
need to transmit as strong a radio signal. They would be more
resistant to radio scanner eavesdropping, have longer battery
life, and be less expensive because the base stations were less
costly. Lastly, digital networks would turn the handset into a
PCS device that could provide a range of services beyond voice
communication, such as e-mail.

When Roth started to beat the "wireless is the future" drum, his audience at first was skeptical. Of the reaction he got, Roth said: "Oh, yeah, people thought I was nuts...they thought, 'My God, this must be a death wish!' But I said, 'No, look at this as an opportunity.'"[10] What Roth saw was that the shift to digital in wireless networks would move the value from the radio technology to the switching technology. Since the size of the cells would be much smaller, the switches would have to work harder to hand off more calls as users traveled across cells. This and exploding growth in the subscriber base would create a more demanding requirement on the switching part of the network.

Roth saw that established suppliers in wireless were strong in radio but still weak in switches. So they were vulnerable. Or as Roth declared:

> ...the people who were in the business were quite ineffectual in the switching part, and I said, this industry is about to go through a discontinuity...this whole industry's going to go from a technology that is perceived as being really intensive on radios to a system where the dominant value will be in the switch. We're good at switches. And we can learn how to build radios...we'll learn how to build radios before they learn how to make switches, so we're going to win.[11]

The year 1992 was a busy one for Roth as he pushed forward with a full-scale launch into the wireless PCS market. He augmented in-house capabilities with acquisitions, joint ventures, and construction of new manufacturing facilities. A centerpiece was the joint venture negotiated with Motorola Inc. then the world's largest maker of cellular phones. The joint venture was to draw upon the strengths of both, with Motorola providing expertise in radio and Nortel providing expertise in switching. Bell Mobility Cellular placed the first big order, $80 million.

In June 1992, AGT Cellular in Alberta used equipment from the venture to set up the first commercial digital cellular service in North America.

The Motorola agreement was followed by the acquisition of the assets of the cellular radio systems division of Calgary-based Novatel and the investment of $12 million to establish a wireless development center in Calgary. Then came the acquisition of a minority interest and a strategic alliance with Matra Communications in France. Its expertise in European standard (GSM) radio systems, along with Nortel's in switching, was expected to open many cellular market opportunities in both Europe (where the GSM standard had been adopted) and the United States (where the question of standards had been left to the marketplace).

In the early going, the Wireless Systems Group did not look like it was going to be the best performing product line during Monty's tenure. Just days after the $1-billion loss was revealed in July 1993, Nortel piled on more bad news by announcing that the much-ballyhooed joint venture with Motorola was coming apart after just eighteen months in operation. The three-year agreement to jointly sell each other's radio cellular products was to be dissolved, sending sales and support staff back to their respective parent companies. Company officials, however, took pains to note that the other aspect of the joint venture—the agreement to jointly develop a system combining Nortel's cellular digital switch with Motorola's radio frequency technology—was still alive.

The cause for the breakup on the marketing and support side of the agreement was the discovery that customers preferred to deal directly with sales people from the parent companies rather than with the sales force of the joint venture. Another reason was different technological visions of the cellular market:

the two companies could not agree on which of the several technical standards in the market they should back in their joint marketing and service efforts.

Nevertheless, the Wireless Systems Group pushed on. In the fall of 1993, Nortel officially launched its line of digital cordless telephones for the business enterprise market in Canada under the brand name of Companion. An early version of PCS devices, the pocket-size phones functioned as a kind of "wireless PBX," allowing employees to take their phones with them as they moved about the workplace.

Roth was promoted to the presidency of the new operating group, Nortel North America, in early 1994. Taking over for Roth in wireless systems was David Twyver, who had been vice president of cellular systems. Besides the wireless PBX product, he inherited an impressive portfolio of wireless products that placed Nortel at the cusp of a major growth trajectory.

One product in the portfolio was the DMS-MTX SuperNode cellular switch, which, upgraded in 1993, remained the largest capacity switch for routing calls over cellular networks. Another was the ServiceBuilder Node, a switch that provided special utilities such as personal numbers and integrated voice/fax on handsets. A third was the Dual Mode base stations, which were proprietary products that gave cellular phone users freedom to roam further afield because of the ability to switch between analog and digital.

A fourth was the SmartAntenna, a directional beam antenna technology acquired from STC PLC and subsequently refined by Nortel. The antenna was particularly attractive because it had the capacity to lock onto and track PCS handsets, which enabled wireless networks to be built with larger cell sizes and fewer base stations. This more efficient solution not only reduced total construction costs by nearly half, but improved the quality of signals (interference from other radio sources was reduced radically).

A fifth and last product was the fixed wireless system, sold under the label of Proximity. In this system, phones were fixed to one location as in wired systems, but were linked to trunk lines by wireless methods. As such, fixed wireless products would be attractive to less-developed countries because national telephone systems could be rolled out more quickly and cheaply. Fixed wireless systems would also be in demand in developed countries as a way for long-distance carriers to bypass local carriers when deregulation of local telephone markets occurred.

A replay of sorts to the Digital World success was in the offing—another case of being in the right place at the right time. For as Nortel was readying its charge into wireless, the regulatory framework was evolving in a way that would boost demand immensely. Namely, the FCC was about to auction off parts of the radio spectrum that would allow PCS networks to be set up. In awarding licenses to the various applicants to operate systems, the FCC would be creating overnight a tidal wave in demand for wireless infrastructure equipment. Nortel, with its strong line up in leading-edge wireless products was superbly positioned to score big gains.

By the end of 1995, a three-stage auction by the FCC had handed out hundreds of licenses to operate at the new frequencies, and garnered about $9 billion for the US Treasury. The first stage of the auction netted $600 million for licenses to provide PCS-based (two-way) paging services. The second stage, the auctioning off of 102 broadband PCS licenses, generated over $7 billion. The third stage sold off narrowband licenses for regional "basic trading" areas to small businesses and minority groups with preferential bidding rights.

As PCS licenses were awarded in America and other countries, orders for PCS equipment started to pour in for Nortel. The company was well placed to reap a bonanza: it had probably what was the most comprehensive and powerful product offering in PCS. Another trump card was the fact that many of the US regional telephone companies were leery of buying wireless equipment from AT&T's manufacturing arm (which had not yet been spun off) since AT&T was a direct competitor in providing wireless services.

One of the first big orders, for $100 million worth of equipment, was placed by BellSouth Corp., the largest of the US regional telephone companies. A $200-million multiyear contract signed with Western Wireless and an upgrading of an order from Omnipoint Corp. to $250 million were some of the other highlights in wireless business generated over the summer and fall of 1995. All in all, it was quite a sweep in the beginning: the first seven equipment orders for PCS networks in the United States went to Nortel.

The largest holder of PCS licenses, Sprint Spectrum, gave Nortel an order for $1 billion worth of PCS infrastructure equipment in early 1996. Although a very large requisition, it was just part of the equipment required for the huge PCS network planned for rollout across the United States over the next two years. Rival AT&T also received a good portion of the business—a larger portion, in fact. Nevertheless, it was still a big win for Nortel, especially since it would generate sales in the North American (CDMA) standard where Nortel had a relatively weak presence.

What really was key in winning the Sprint Spectrum contract was Nortel's willingness to agree to Sprint's criteria for vendor financing (lending them the money to buy their goods). Vendor financing is not unusual in the telecommunication industry, but Sprint Spectrum was demanding terms more aggressive than usual. Besides wanting suppliers to finance most of the construction, installation, and maintenance, Sprint wanted to stretch out repayment over thirteen years and not have to make any payments until three or four years after the start of operations. The other main rival in the running, Motorola, was either unwilling or unable to agree to the financing terms and so did not receive any major contracts from Sprint. European rivals such as Ericsson were shut out because they were not supporting the CDMA standard.

The vendor financing for Sprint Spectrum further raised concerns about the risks taken on by Nortel and AT&T's manufacturing subsidiary (soon to be spun off as Lucent Technologies). With so many PCS deals up for tender all at once, and commercial banks uneasy about financing an unproven technology, the two telecommunication firms had been aggressive in winning business by offering attractive loans to customers, and, consequently, a large amount of vendor financing debt was accumulating on their balance sheets. Analysts and consultants began to raise their concerns in meetings with company executives.

Nortel was already concerned on its own. Allowing for the possibility of default, it set up reserves of over $50 million in 1996. Another tactic pursued was negotiations with financial institutions to have them take over some of the credits, and in May 1997, the negotiations met with success. A syndicate of twenty financial institutions, led by the Bank of America, agreed to assume $1.7 billion, or 80 percent, of Nortel's vendor debt. These were the first PCS-based vendor loans that were laid off to commercial lenders.

While the debt rollover plan was under negotiation, Nortel's wireless equipment product line received an endorsement from an unexpected source. For over ten years, the company had been shut out in sales to AT&T, which naturally purchased equipment from its manufacturing arm. But in the fall of 1996, AT&T Wireless signed an agreement to buy over $1 billion of Nortel's PCS products.

AT&T Wireless said it picked Nortel because its cordless phone for use in work settings was better than any other on the market. The company's intention was to combine Nortel's wireless PBX system with its own PCS phone system so that customers could use the same phone both inside and outside the office (rather than the current practice of using one for inside and one for outside).

The contribution of the wireless portfolio to sales and earnings growth was quite significant over the 1990s. It was, indeed, the fastest-growing line of the four major products groups, beating out public carrier, enterprise, and transmission networks. The explanation for the remarkable performance was, in part, that the wireless product line was riding a strong tailwind as market demand soared due to changes in the regulatory and market environments. Still, the Wireless Systems Group, set up by Roth and subsequently led by Twyver, must be given its due for latching onto those tailwinds. Roth, in particular, foresaw the opportunities and set in motion the development of a leading-edge product portfolio at just the right time.

11

The Vision Thing

Webtone

The challenge of leadership throughout the ages has been to win the commitment and best efforts of those in the ranks. The degree of cooperation can range along a continuum from open rebellion to fervent adherence. In open rebellion, people engage in counterproductive behavior or even sabotage. In the middle of the continuum, people are accepting of the leadership but are indifferent and often seek self-fulfillment in outside activities. At the fervent adherence end, people identify with the organization and are happily devoted to achievement within its framework.

Effective leadership, say historians and management experts, involves a unique combination of circumstance and personality. The circumstance usually is a situation of crisis or opportunity, and the leaders tend to be persons who articulate the concerns of the group and provide a goal or vision to light the way. The more compelling the vision, the greater the creativity and energy unleashed throughout the group.

In the months leading up to his elevation to chief executive officer, John Roth pondered the direction of the telecommunication industry and what his company would have to do to continue growing. Over and over, one emerging grand discontinuity kept coming to mind: the Internet. The more he thought about it, the more he was convinced that it was going to sweep the industry. Indeed, it was going to sweep society at large, bringing about revolutionary changes in the way business and communication were carried out. "The Internet changes everything." he said.[1]

By the time Roth assumed the helm at Nortel, the massive ramifications of the Internet were quite apparent to him. E-mail was going to alter patterns of communication dramatically. Online commerce was going to have serious implications for bricks-and-mortar retailers, wholesalers, brokers, and other old-fashioned middlemen. Newspapers, television, radio and other mass media would have to converge, at least in part, on the Internet. Telemedicine and teleeducation would become new realities. Long-anticipated services such as video-on-demand and videoconferencing would finally become practical. Web site design and consultancy would flourish. The list goes on.

But at the same time, Roth was also aware of several shortcomings in the delivery of the Internet. Users often complained of a variety of inconveniences. Establishing a connection was sometimes a problem. And once logged on, most residential users could not receive or send telephone calls. Flipping through Web pages was annoying when display of text and graphics took anywhere from a few seconds to a few minutes to load (jokesters liked to say WWW stood for World Wide Wait). Downloading software was particularly bad, in some cases requiring more than an hour of waiting. Video images were jerky, and audio was sometimes choppy or tinny. Online shoppers worried about the security and privacy of their transactions. Then there were the periodic interruptions and system crashes.

Some two months into his new job, on December 3, 1997, Roth sent an e-mail to the 74,000 employees at Nortel. Called "The Right Angle Turn," the memorandum outlined a strategy for capitalizing on the opportunities raised by the Internet— for turning Nortel into a leading developer and supplier of Internet products and infrastructure. He sent out the message because he wanted to get his company focused on the Internet. As he said, "I wanted to challenge our troops by asking them the question, 'What is the role for [Nortel] with the growth of the World Wide Web?'"[2]

In the memo, he outlined a vision, called "Webtone," for making the Internet as fast and as reliable to use as the telephone. The Web part of his label represented the shimmering potential of the Internet as a major driver for human communication in the twenty-first century. The tone part of the phrase represented the ubiquitous, automatic, and reliable nature of the dial tone on the telephone system. In short, Roth was outlining a mission to combine the best features of the Internet and the telephone system, or on another level, data networks with telecommunication networks. To do so, Nortel would have to make a right-angle turn and plunge full scale into a relatively new field. He wanted the troops to understand the direction the corporation was going to pursue and to issue a challenge to find ways of implementing the shift.

With a culture of change now permeating the corporation (thanks to the reigns of Lobb, Light, Stern, and others), the response from the ranks was like a finely tuned roadster. Nortel's employees rose to Roth's challenge and came forward with ideas and suggestions that Roth himself felt had improved upon his original thinking. He had been mainly focused on redirecting the product portfolio toward the vast opportunities in the Internet, of getting the company Web-centric so that design engineers, marketing staff, and everyone else would start to evaluate what they were doing with reference to its potential for the Web. But out of his challenge came a move from the grassroots and middle ranks to fashion a "culture of speed," a striving to reduce the long product development cycles typical of the telecommunication industry to be more in tune with the fast-paced environment of the Internet.

Webtone outlined several specific opportunities. One particular business opportunity was improving access to the Internet. An example of a Nortel product aimed at this was the Megabit modem, which allows users to enjoy always-on and high-speed Internet connections over telephone lines. A second opportunity was developing integrated Web applications. An example of a Nortel product addressing this area was Internet Call Waiting, which enables single-line users to tell if they are receiving a telephone call while on the Internet. A third opportunity was developing wireless access to the Internet, which was more of a longer-term project but seen to be potentially vast by the middle of the 2000s. Finally, a fourth opportunity was increasing the capacity, expandability, and reliability of Internet transmission, which Nortel was doing through products such as the TransportNode family of optical carrier systems.

The turn to the Internet was actually not new within Nortel. Indeed, Roth's predecessor, Monty, had earlier outlined an Internet strategy and approved the development of several Internet-related products. A better manager than wordsmith, Monty had rendered his version somewhat obscure by saying Nortel intended "to supply networks with reliable, user friendly, and controlled access to information, entertainment, and the evolving electronic marketplace."[3] Roth, a much better conceptualist, crystallized the new direction by reducing it to one word: "Webtone." Naming your corporate vision may seem a trifling matter, but in an age in which the name of a Web site can be worth millions of dollars, the impact of such a detail should not be underestimated.

Webtone, in any event, was a vision that not only outlined a new corporate direction but also conveyed to employees, customers, and investors alike just how Nortel would add value—how it would differentiate itself from Cisco and other competitors. Coming from the data networking industry, Cisco was claiming to be a "New World" company, one of the few equipped for building the Internet. It said that companies such as Nortel were from the "Old World," laggards in meeting the needs of a new era.

Webtone, however, was a vision that went a step further than the Cisco portrayal. It highlighted the instability, unreliability, and quality problems in using data communication systems, while identifying Nortel as the company preparing to address these problems. In short, Nortel was moving more quickly to provide the bounty of the Internet in conjunction with the transmission quality of the telephone system. In the important battle for mindshare, Webtone appeared to be a victory.

The vision had to be enunciated. It was not possible to stay put and do nothing, since the perils of ignoring the Internet could be disastrous for Nortel. Roth was aware how traffic from the Internet and other data networks was surpassing voice traffic on the public telephone network. From virtually nothing in the early 1970s, data traffic had soared to over 50 percent of transmissions by 1997. And it was growing at a pace of 30 to 40 percent per year, meaning that in a matter of a few years, data would be at least 80 percent of the messages carried on the network.

Circuit-based telephone networks hence appeared destined to be displaced by data networks, given that the latter were more efficient at carrying data, voice, and video traffic. Circuit-based networks hold a dedicated circuit open during a transmission, and some transmission capacity lies unused during idle periods in Internet or telephone usage. Packet-based networks, on the other hand, chop up multimedia messages into packets and sends them intermingled down the transmission channel altogether, making better use of transmission capacity.

As such, Nortel's traditional digital switches for central office and PBX markets faced eventual obsolescence. Therefore, Webtone had to succeed. Much more was at stake than missing some opportunities to do a repeat of the wireless initiative from the early 1990s. The survival of Nortel itself was in the balance. The years ahead were going to be either Nortel's best or worst. "The transformation from traditional switch technology to data networks is a revolution we have to win," Roth told a reporter. "We win it, or we die."[4]

Less than a year into the right-angle turn, Webtone ran headlong into an iceberg, sending a violent shudder deep down into the bowels of the ship. A momentary silence ensued as the shock settled in. Then voices rose from all around, asking if the damage was serious. Was the vessel taking on water? Further on into the turmoil, calls were heard to replace those responsible. A senior executive or two would have to go. Captain Roth himself was a prime candidate, and his vision appeared headed toward an early demise.

The day was September 28, 1998. The place was Essex House in New York. Nortel was holding its annual meeting with Wall Street analysts. The company had just issued a news release reaffirming the financial forecast for the next three years, which was for annual revenue growth of 14 percent. But there was some confusion about whether or not the figures included the recently acquired Bay Networks. On the break, Nortel executives were approached for clarification. That was when the chief financial officer, Wes Scott, sensing the need to set the details straight for the whole room, jumped back up onto the stage. This tiniest of deeds was to have severe repercussions for both him and Nortel.

He said that Nortel's third-quarter revenue growth with Bay Networks would be "in the high teens" as forecast in the news release, and would be in the "low teens" without Bay Networks. Nothing dramatic in this statement—or so it seemed. The audience somehow misinterpreted it to be a retreat on the forecast in the press release, that the bullish story for public consumption was being moderated. Some saw the statement as an admission that the Bay merger was not working out. Others thought they heard the company say it would not meet its projections for the next two years.

An analyst on the scene gave his perspective on the pandemonium breaking out:

> It culminated with [the] chief financial officer getting up on stage and saying "Here's our expectations for the year, but that second-half ramp-up we were looking for ain't happening, and a couple of other things aren't going quite right." Then he got offstage and he was just descended upon. I don't think we ever saw him again. A few phones flipped open and within thirty seconds the stock was trading down.[5]

On the heels of the confusing financial picture, Nortel's stock plunged 15 percent before trading was halted around noon. The next day, when trading reopened, the pounding continued. By the close, the share price was down again for a two-day drop of nearly 25 percent. In following days, the price drifted even lower. In all, market capitalization on the Toronto Stock Exchange was reduced $9 billion (Canadian) as a result of the incident. Said one shaken observer, "It was only twelve words. That works out to $750 million a word."[6]

The confusion had led many angry analysts to quickly downgrade their financial forecasts. A survey by First Call Corp. revealed that fifteen of twenty-five analysts had reduced their numbers. The consensus projection for earnings slipped to 38 cents a share for the third quarter and to $1.82 a share for the fiscal year. In both cases, this was one cent less than the previous projections. Such is the emotionalism found in technology stocks that a one cent downgrade in earnings erases $9 billion of the value of a company's stock.

Of course, the plunge did not happen just out of the blue. A cloud of apprehension had been building since the takeover of Bay Networks several months before. And the tone in stock markets in the summer and fall of 1998 was quite bearish because of the fear that the global economy would be dragged into deflation by collapsing Asian economies. Finally, the week before, a large European telecommunication equipment firm had issued an earnings warning that destroyed nearly a quarter of its equity value.

Still, the market overreacted to Nortel's bungled presentation. When Nortel later reported third-quarter earnings, the company came out just as they said they would. There was 20 percent revenue growth including Bay Networks in the tally, and 12 percent growth excluding Bay Networks. To those investors who kept their heads, it was an excellent opportunity to buy Nortel stock at a tremendous discount.

Over ensuing months, the price of Nortel stock rebounded strongly on a steady progression of good news from the corporation. One big lift came in early March 1999 when a breakthrough with AT&T was achieved. The latter conglomerate was under pressure to upgrade its telephone network to accommodate burgeoning Internet traffic. This would require shifting Internet traffic off onto a data packet network and purchasing a new set of packet-based switches.

But in early 1999, AT&T announced that it was doing just such an evaluation on Nortel's packet-based switches. The actual order came a few months later, for $300 million worth of Nortel's DMS-500 switches. It was not a terribly huge order in terms of dollars, but it was in terms of psychological significance to the company and investors. It indicated that Nortel was starting to make inroads into the huge AT&T market. AT&T was signaling a willingness to break with its preferential purchasing habits, and Nortel was emerging as a key provider to its next generation network. Now, Lucent did not look so intimidating.

Soon after the AT&T news, it was announced that Nortel would team up with three technology giants—Hewlett-Packard, Intel, and Microsoft—in a research and development alliance aimed at upgrading the Meridian and Norstar PBXs for small and medium-sized businesses. The alliance would deliver integrated voice and data service, integrated messaging, and Internet-enabled call centers. An open system would be used, comprising Intel hardware, Microsoft Windows NT 4.0 operating software, and Hewlett Packard's computer servers. By forming this partnership, Nortel was moving to defend its hold on the PBX market against the integrated voice and data products from Cisco and Lucent.

Shortly afterward, a megadeal was announced with British Telecommunications to build the world's largest Internet telephony network. Daily newspapers hailed it as the first practical manifestation of Webtone. Located in Spain, the network would cost more than $1.5 billion. Once completed, it would provide instant and reliable access to the Internet and other media. Voice signals on the packet-based network would be digitized and transported with packets of other media.

Later in the spring of 1999, more gains in Nortel's capitalization resulted from supply agreements signed with some regional telephone companies. One deal worth $1 billion over five years was signed with Bell Atlantic, which until then had not been a big customer. It was also one of the largest orders to date for Nortel's high-speed local-access gear. Webtone was showing signs of life, with Nortel emerging as the supplier of choice for telephone carriers wishing to solve bottleneck problems on the local loop. A second supply agreement, worth $5 billion over 10 years, reaffirmed a long-standing relationship with Bell South.

While announcements of blockbuster contracts helped produce a rebound for Nortel shares, so did growth in quarterly earnings and revenues above the expectations of brokerage analysts. The financial improvement originated from what had once been the sleepiest part of Nortel: transmission products. The contribution was indeed substantial; over the four years to 1999, revenues from the transmission systems division rose from $600 million to $5 billion, reaching 22 percent of total company sales.

Within the transmission products division, the accelerating product line was fiber-optic systems. This escalation was in response to the mounting demand for extra transmission capacity to accommodate the increasing volumes of multimedia traffic. Thus, in the early stages, Webtone was actually a beneficiary of a vision announced in 1989—FiberWorld. The many initiatives and acquisitions launched by Roth in 1998 were still in a transition phase, their main contribution to the bottom line not expected to come until after 2000.

The goods news and financial results combined to push Nortel shares up virtually without pause over 1999. The extent was truly impressive—more than a fourfold gain from the trough in the fall of 1998 to the end of 1999. Webtone crashed into an iceberg and made ice cubes. Now it was steaming full speed ahead, illustrating how the brokerage analysts can get it wrong sometimes. If the market gets caught up in an emotional wave of panic selling, that just creates a buying opportunity for canny investors. This is even more likely the case if the collapse wipes out several billion dollars in market capitalization on an earnings downgrade of one cent per share.

Turning on a Dime

In the technology industry, success is often a matter of being the first to market with a new product. A superior model, the best customer-support apparatus, and other goodies may not matter much if another company has already locked up customers. There is a tendency for clients to stay with the company that first introduced a new item, and to win them away requires a lot more time and money than if a company were there first.

Fully aware of the merits of being first to market and how the fast-paced markets of data communication did not allow for in-house development of products in time, chief executive Roth embarked upon a major program of acquisitions to position his company as a leading supplier of Webtone networks. It was a bold gambit. Among the dangers was the possibility of ending up with some duds or of having key staff in the acquired companies desert the ship.

On the other hand, companies like Cisco were enjoying great success with a steady series of acquisitions. A kind of self-perpetuating dynamic seemed to be in place in which a steadily appreciating stock price was used as currency to finance takeovers of other companies via all-stock deals. They added no debt and siphoned off little cash, so they were a relatively painless and inexpensive way to expand. Dilution of equity would be offset by ever-rising profits. Moreover, the steadily rising share price was a great way to smooth over the problems associated with integrating the takeovers. Nortel had enjoyed a steady progression in its stock value since 1993, and it had perhaps overlooked its potential as a competitive tool. Once Roth became chief executive, that all changed.

During the first three years of Roth's tenure as chief executive, Nortel purchased fourteen companies at a cost of $22 billion. Many were start-up firms with revolutionary technology. To spot these acquisition opportunities, Roth set up a team within Nortel to invest in venture capital funds such as Accel Partners of Palo Alto. The point was not so much to make money as to get close to the origin of disruptive technologies. "Investing in venture capital funds allows us to get our nose under the tent and gain much earlier awareness about new companies and technologies," said one of the managers of the venture capital investments program.[1]

Concerning the challenge of retaining key staff from the acquired companies, Nortel constructed deals where the "earnout" was tied to market milestones so that payment occurred not when the acquisition was done but when certain objectives were reached. That bought time for a smooth transition; the principals were given incentives to stay and make sure the acquisition was a success. It also gave Nortel time to bolster the team with some long-term Nortel employees who would step up and fill the shoes of any departing staff after the transition period was over.

Under Roth, Nortel was getting to be quite experienced at acquisitions. As Roth stated:

> Now, this is turning out to be a formula for us. We are almost at the point of "productizing" how we assimilate companies. We've done fourteen or so of them so far. It takes practice to do these things, and we are getting a lot of practice these days![2]

$$\maltese$$

Not all the ideas for acquisitions originated from the venture capital investment team. A case in point was the biggest acquisition—Bay Networks Inc. When the deal was consummated in 1998, Nortel paid over $7 billion for what was the third-largest member of the US data communication industry (behind Cisco and Ascend). Bay would give Nortel a broad range of products for corporate data networks, which, along with existing PBX and related products, would allow Nortel to offer the broadest array of voice and data products in the corporate market. Nortel would now be the company in a better position to serve as a one-stop shop, sparing customers the inconvenience of going to three or four vendors to assemble systems.

Bay Networks would add $2 billion in sales and 7,000 people to the payroll, increasing the total work force to 80,000. It would bring expertise in router technology and data packet networks, particularly in the LAN segment in which Nortel had little penetration. Nortel was strong in the WAN segment of enterprise data networks, but given that WAN customer needs originated in the LAN area, Nortel was at a competitive disadvantage without a presence to tap early into emerging trends. Another benefit of the Bay deal would be that its routers could be integrated with Nortel's technologies, resulting in integrated voice and data IP networks for the enterprise and carrier markets. It was a giant step toward implementing Webtone.

Spurring Roth into action was the realization that convergence of the data communication and telecommunication industries was inevitable. Given the scenario about to unfold, it would be better to be the first one in with a cross-industry merger. The first to buy would have its pick of the crop and could avoid paying a premium before a flurry of merger activity pushed up prices. Being first off the mark would also be a way of differentiating Nortel from the other telecommunication firms. For a time, it would be the only one working toward integrated voice and data networks, capturing important mindshare with customers. Nortel would also get an earlier start on melding the two technologies and possibly end up ahead in the product development curve.

It was indeed obvious to Roth that a period of mergers was around the corner (an expectation later confirmed by Lucent's takeover of Ascend and Cisco's of Cerent). In addition to traffic trends on telephone networks, there were other signals. Cisco was laying down the gauntlet in announcing its plans to snatch away PBX and carrier clients from the lumbering telecommunication giants. And just before the Bay deal was done, Sprint woke up telecom equipment suppliers with the announcement that it would build a new carrier network based on data packet transmission, which meant that it would no longer be ordering circuit switches for its network.

The investment community, however, was not yet sold on the direction in which Roth was going. Nortel's share price plunged over 15 percent in heavy trading on the day news of the Bay takeover broke. Some analysts thought the price paid was too high, while others (still not fully aware of how disruptive the Internet was going to be) believed the Bay operations would distract Nortel from its traditional business. Still other analysts expressed concern over Nortel's ability to make the transition from voice to converged networks, where shorter product development cycles would require a degree of nimbleness uncharacteristic of large telecommunication companies. The problem of successfully integrating two different corporate cultures was another worry, compounded by the suspicion that the wrong data networking company had been purchased, a second-rate player whose earnings and sales were slipping. In short, there were a great many uncertainties swirling about in the wake of the takeover.

Perhaps most weighty of the analysts' concerns was the perception that the wrong data networking company had been bought. Bay Networks was seen as a troubled company from the time it was first formed in 1994 from the merger of SynOptics Communications Inc. and Wellfleet Communications Inc. The two did not mesh well together, and the combination was apparently rife with internal conflicts. Leadership, it was said, was lacking for a time; decisions were not taken to provide direction. Following the merger, ground was lost to Cisco, as evidenced by declining profitability. A new chief executive, ex-Intel executive David House, was subsequently brought in to restructure the company. He was into his second year when Nortel came along and bought it.

Roth justified his move by pointing out that there was very little overlap in product lines between Bay and Nortel. As such, Nortel would not be paying extra for products it did not need, and the integration process afterward would be a lot easier since there would be no need for large-scale cutbacks and layoffs. Nearly all the other data networking firms had overlap with Nortel. Moreover, Cisco, a company with a market capitalization over twice that of Nortel's, was virtually impossible to buy. Not that it mattered: CEO Chambers was not interested in amalgamating. And the number-two data networking firm, Ascend Communications, would have been expensive to buy as well. Meanwhile, Bay was on the cheap side because of its perceived problems—problems that Roth believed could be remedied.

Roth further mentioned that when he went shopping for a data networking company, he noticed that Bay routers were the closest to the reliability requirements outlined in the Webtone vision. In data communication systems in which continuous uptime was a high priority, as in the transfer of financial data within the banking community, he found that Bay routers were used. Other users were the New York Stock Exchange and large manufacturers that used Bay equipment in their backup "last resort" systems. These Bay customers valued the multiple processors in the company's router. If a processor were to fail, the Bay router did not fail completely—it just lost some capacity. Higher-priority traffic still would go through. The data network used by the New York Stock Exchange, for example, was setting the benchmark with an uptime of 99.998 percent.

In months following the acquisition, senior Nortel executives, with the agreement of outside observers, declared that the integration of the two companies was going smoothly. One senior executive involved in the integration process expressed a degree of surprise at just how well it was all going. By getting the two warring factions of the company to shift their focus onto the external challenge of meeting customer needs, he was pleased to note that performance was advancing noticeably. Helping out with the process was tight management of the transition period; little was left to chance. Integration teams were created, which got groups of Bay and Nortel employees focused on solving the adjustment problems. Another measure was the establishment of an immediate and continuous flow of communication between the two organizations so that employees at all levels would be kept informed and rumors could be dispelled.

Roth added another perspective on why the merger was turning out to be a success:

> I saw inside Bay a lot of practices that had been brought in from Intel…and these practices were closer to the mark than what we had been doing. So we took those practices and put them across the corporation, like bonus treatments and how we rewarded people and how we measured our progress in R&D. The shock for the folks at Bay was not really what it could have been if we had imposed a lot of Nortel's practices.[3]

At the annual meeting held on May 1, 1997, Roth told shareholders and reporters:

> Manufacturing is becoming less and less of what we do…. It's more in the area of assembling silicon parts and writing software code. We no longer describe ourselves as a manufacturer. We consider ourselves as an integrator of networks….[4]

So a less-trumpeted aspect of the Webtone vision was that Nortel's contribution would be not so much as a manufacturer of Internet infrastructure but more as a systems integrator—a company that packages its own products with others to provide systems that address customer needs. A few months later, Roth left no doubt how he saw Nortel's role in bringing Webtone networks to fruition:

> We don't just want to be a manufacturer of hardware where shipping more out the door is important. We are more of a systems integrator putting together networks....[5]

An important corollary of this viewpoint was the need to be involved with the customer. Designing for the Web, as Roth declared, is like trying to hit a moving target; it is difficult to anticipate where it is going. The only way to do it is to "be engaged, to break through to the end customer somehow...."[6] Like any good systems integrator, therefore, Nortel had to be close to the customer, to get a communication channel opened up in which Nortel learned about customer needs and problems as they arose. Then, Nortel's role was to take that feedback and provide solutions at the earliest stage possible.

The launching of several small Web-related products in late 1997—particularly the Megabit modem, the voice button for Web sites, and Internet call waiting—were derided by some observers as window dressing, as a superficial attempt by a stodgy old telecom player to capture a Web aura. As one analyst put it, "It's showing you can play the hip crowd, like that U2 video where you have these guys in their 40s wearing disco clothes. I cringe."[7] But according to Roth, these preliminary sorties into the Internet realm had a definite purpose, which was to commence relationships with a new set of customers. The important thing was to get started on a process of communication as a way to help guide the design process.

In defining Nortel as a triple-S firm—that is, one focused on software, silicon, and systems integration—Roth was stating that these were the areas of strength for the company. They were what it did best. By implication, corporate resources should be allocated to them; Nortel should specialize in its natural advantages and get out of areas over which it had no particular mastery. The first substantial steps toward putting theory into practice came in the middle of 1999 with the announcement that Nortel would sell off eight of its manufacturing plants for $400 million and close down two more. About 2,300 employees would go with the plants to their new owners, with whom Nortel had signed supply agreements for the products formerly produced in-house.

Projected cost savings from this and future efforts at outsourcing and rationalization of manufacturing were $250 to $300 million per year. All of Nortel's twenty-four manufacturing plants would be touched in one way or another as the company shifted from being a manufacturer of hardware to an integrator of systems. The freed-up resources would be available to help finance levels of employment and research in mission-critical.

An integral part of providing customer solutions was becoming more of a marketing and advertising company. An article in *Red Herring* magazine in October 1998 pointed out that Nortel had been lacking in this department. It compared Cisco, Lucent, and Nortel to the *Seinfeld* episode that reduced the Three Tenors to Pavarotti, Domingo, and "the other guy"—the latter being Nortel's position in the trio. Cisco and Lucent had "world-class marketing engines that have taken them the extra mile...."[8]

Roth began to work on this deficiency with the launch in March 1999 of the first phase of a $100-million mass advertising campaign to brand Nortel as an Internet company, featuring television ads playing the Beatles tune, *Come Together*. The second phase was launched in September 1999 and asked the question, "What do you want the Internet to be?" The TV and print ads mentioned how Nortel was building a high-performance Internet and encouraged people to send in their suggestions. Some of the responses received were featured in the third phase of the ad campaign, which kicked off in January 2000.

⁂

Successful corporations tend to keep on doing what made them strong, and therein lies their Achilles heel. For when conditions change in the external environment, applying the success formula of the past may no longer be appropriate. Concentrating on pumping out more and better products within its area of expertise, the corporation may miss growth opportunities that assure survival.

The initial reaction Roth received while advocating a line of wireless communication products in 1990 illustrates why technology companies sometimes fail. In response to his proposal, a senior executive said (in Roth's words): "Nortel doesn't know anything about wireless. Its not switching-intensive. It's mostly radios, and we are not good at radios."[9] But, fortunately, Roth won his case eventually. Nortel transferred some resources away from its core competency and let Roth and his wireless division learn a new skill. If they had not, Nortel may not have recovered its growth dynamic after the debacle of 1993.

Rather than being a core competency-focused company seeking to offer products with all the bells and whistles, Roth wanted Nortel to be an opportunity-focused company that moved quickly to capitalize on discontinuities. To those who sought to continue strengthening an existing product line, he said "Fine, but what else have you learned lately?"[10] Just as the concept of continuous learning was accepted for individuals, Roth believed a similar concept was necessary for corporations. Building a core competency was important, but then the corporation needed to keep asking itself, What else are we well positioned to learn quicker than other companies?

To move Nortel toward his concept of a fast-moving and opportunity-focused corporation, Roth embarked on a dramatic reorganization, after his appointment as president of North American operations in 1994 and chief operating officer in 1995. Before, Nortel was organized by function, with marketing, product management, research, and other functions operating independently. There were a variety of subsidiaries, ranging from BNR for research to Nortel International for foreign sales. Coordinating it all from headquarters was corporate staff, which set spending priorities.

Roth scrapped this entire structure and set up a new one based on lines of businesses serving types of customers: carrier (e.g., AT&T), wireless (e.g., AT&T Wireless), and enterprise (e.g., CitiCorp) groups. Within these lines of business were thirty-five or so product groups headed by general managers. The geographical and functional subsidiaries were disassembled, and their operations were integrated under the respective general managers of the product groupings.

As such, the general managers would have more autonomy, like the managers of high-technology start-ups. This was a decentralization of decision making aimed at speeding up reaction time to market opportunities. With all the required resources under their direct control, the general managers would be able to move quicker; they would not have to postpone actions while going through a round of meetings with various functional entities and headquarters to secure the necessary permissions and resources.

The integration of BNR with the business lines was particularly significant. It placed research staff closer to the customer so that they would be more sensitive to evolving needs in the marketplace when designing new technologies. And situated near the front lines, they would more easily be able to adopt the alpha-beta design process, whereby a simple version of the product is created and put in front of the customer to obtain feedback to complete its development.

Integrating research and development with the business units would furthermore help bring an end to the delays caused by disputes over what products to make and what their designs should be. When BNR was in existence, Roth felt the stalemates over such matters ate up too much time. Customers were left in the lurch for too long because the corporation was focused on internal issues.

As a result of dismantling BNR, each of the business lines was assigned a vice president for technology. In addition to providing leadership for new products in their respective lines, they would also be responsible for formulating Nortel's overall technology strategy and embedding future technology road maps into the strategic and operating plans of the company. That would involve "seeking out innovative technology, both internally and externally, and anticipating the discontinuities in the market that create opportunities."[11]

All in all, Roth undertook a radical reengineering of Nortel's organizational structure. The embracing of the change by the rank and file is in contrast to the Stern era. One factor that may have helped was that the changes took place when considerable appreciation in the share price was occurring, which enhanced employee holdings in the company share plan. Another factor may have been that Nortel employees, having been through so much change in previous years, were imbued with a culture of change. As well, Roth used the reorganizations to fill the upper ranks with managers who shared his viewpoint. As one analyst said, "He managed to basically eliminate anyone who was not loyal to him."[12]

✤

In the mid-1990s, on a Nortel campus in Georgia, Jack Terry was developing a packet-based technology that would enable voice and data communication to travel over local loops at rates up to 200 times faster than the average household modem. But he was worried that the bureaucracy, focused on its core competency in circuit-based systems, might kill off the project (he had found from his experience over the previous two decades that managers of large corporations tended to have a mind-set of sticking with what they knew best).

This time, however, he decided to bypass several layers in the corporation and went directly to the vice president of customer network solutions. The latter was in charge of a discretionary fund from which seed money could be handed out to projects off the beaten path. The vice president could give out several hundred thousand dollars if he so desired, without any questions asked from above. In a sense, he was playing the role of a venture capitalist, but he was taking his risks within the confines of a large corporation.

Successful in obtaining funding, Terry built a prototype and set up a small unit within Nortel to do field trials and product demonstrations. At one of those presentations, he convinced a divisional president of the merits of his idea and received financing of several million dollars from a discretionary fund under his control. Terry began to report directly to the president. That way, the president would be able to keep tabs on his investment as well as keep Terry out of the clutches of middle managers who might scuttle the initiative.

Once his product was ready to be launched, Terry and his team made a presentation to senior executives, who decided that his project had merit and would probably do well if spun off as a separate company. For one thing, a spin-off would attract stronger partners and financing from external parties. So, in early 1998, Elastic Networks was born and began a process of disengaging from Nortel. A final break came when the new company's employees' names disappeared off the Nortel e-mail and phone system.

Many others have gone through the Terry experience at Nortel. An earlier case was the group behind Entrust Technologies Inc., which specialized in providing secure transactions over computer networks through data encryption, digital certificates, and other methods. Entrust began in 1993 as the Secure Networks division of Nortel, but it was spun off as a separate company through an initial public offering of shares in early 1997. Nortel retained a large equity stake in the company. Regarding the spin-off, a senior Nortel executive said: "We cannot utilize all the ideas we generate. So when we see a viable enterprise, we will explore various options [such as spinning the company off]."[13]

Another spin-off was Channelware Inc., formerly a Nortel unit that designed technology for renting software on a pay-per-use basis. Nortel retained 44 percent ownership in it. Another ex-Nortel unit, Saraide, was a wireless Internet service provider. In late 1999, it was bought by Infospace.com Inc.; investors (including Nortel) received $314 million. Other internal units that have gone (or will go) solo include those developing systems for fraud detection, software evaluation, software repair, and data distribution. Through spin-offs like these, Nortel was eager to show that it is a flexible organization able to offer an outlet for entrepreneurial-minded employees, even if their ideas did not fit in with the corporate product portfolio.

Technology is an ideas business. The history of the technology industry contains many instances of companies with researchers who came up with billion-dollar ideas that were allowed to slip away. Talented employees may leave because the potential of their ideas is rejected or not foreseen. Nortel itself has had its share of misses—of projects it helped to bring along but whose benefits were later expropriated by other companies or former employees in their own companies.

The spin-off program is an attempt to capture some of the benefits emanating from the ideas percolating within the ranks. Retaining a large equity interest in the spin-off, Nortel can either sell it off at a profit or raise its interest to a controlling stake should the marketplace validate the underlying technology. At the same time, the opportunity to use Nortel as a platform to launch a start-up company helped to retain those high-energy individuals who sought rewards greater than a regular paycheck. It is a way, in short, of internalizing an entrepreneurial culture and keeping a large corporate bureaucracy from becoming ossified.

The importance of encouraging risk-taking and openness to different ideas within a large corporation cannot be underestimated. This is particularly true of large technology companies in which disruptive technologies can come out of nowhere to overthrow a competitive edge. In video recorders, VHS crushed Betamax; in music recording, compact discs killed off vinyl records; and in computers, microcomputers vanquished minicomputers. The losers in these technology shifts tended to have structures that reinforced what they did well but were not open to outside technologies.

Minicomputer manufacturers such as Digital Equipment, for example, failed because of a rigid culture that starved embryonic personal computer research projects. Therefore, to help spot and adapt to the disruptive trends at an early stage, alternative and competing solutions within an organization are to be encouraged. In the short term, it may mean higher operating costs, but in the long term, it could be the key to survival. The spin-off program within Nortel represents such a strategy. In other words, it is an attempt to fashion an agile corporation able to cope with upheavals in technology.

13

Trump Card in the Internet Stakes

Fiber Optics

In 1998, Dr. Rudolph Kriegler joined Colin Beaumont as one of the few employees to be awarded the Nortel Fellow Emeritus designation. To earn the prestigious title, both made pioneering contributions to technological innovation at Nortel. Beaumont's role in the development of digital switches helped give Nortel its first big boost; Kriegler's contribution to the development of fiber-optic systems helped put Nortel at the heart of the Internet.

The similarities between the two men mostly end there. Beaumont was the bloody-minded engineer who brought a rugged style to the art of system design, while Kriegler was the gentle scientist who fired only one person during his two decades of managing the development of semiconductor chips and fiber-optic lasers. And whereas Beaumont was in charge of a large-scale mainstream project, Kriegler at times put his own job on the line and undertook unofficial developmental projects to get the fiber-optic product line going within Nortel.

Rudy Kriegler came to Canada after graduating in 1956 with a BSc in physics from the Roland Eotvos University in Budapest, Hungary. He got his master's degree in physics from the University of Toronto in 1958, worked for a while at the Ontario Research Foundation, and returned to the U of T to obtain his PhD in physics (infrared spectroscopy and molecular physics). He did his graduate work under professors who had earlier guided the doctoral work of Donald Chisholm, BNR's first president.

Joining Nortel in 1966, Kriegler went to work in the Physical Sciences Research department. His supervisor gave him free reign to "go and see what he could do to improve"[1] the process for producing semiconductors. Working under this broad mandate within the labs of Nortel over the next dozen years, he gained international recognition for his contributions in the field of microelectronics—authoring twenty-four scientific articles and presenting papers at nearly a dozen technical conferences. Perhaps his most important breakthrough was to find a way to enhance the reliability of metal oxide silicon chips by introducing hydrogen chloride during the production process.

Kriegler's leadership in developing advanced technology resulted in his appointment to the BNR management ranks in 1975. Also a factor in his appointment was an ability to speak with a clarity that made his message easily understood. In accepting managerial responsibilities, he was not motivated so much by the prospect of rising up the corporate hierarchy, but by the fact that he would be in control of his own research shop. Indeed, throughout most of his managerial career, he remained more the scientist than the executive; his disinterest in speaking the "executive language"[2] and playing the political game resulted in the occasional predicament from which he usually extricated himself by delivering results of considerable benefit to the company.

As for managing people under his charge, he turned out to be adept, and generally enjoyed the trust and respect of his staff. There was usually a sense of loyalty within the group, which Kriegler attributed, in part, to "having grown up together over the years at Nortel."[3] Helping to preserve this environment, though, was his dislike for heavy-handed measures. There may have been some persons who should have been disciplined or dismissed, but he found ways to allocate work appropriately within the group.

In 1977, he faced a bit of a challenge when he was promoted to senior manager of the Department of Optoelectronics, an area where he would be applying his skills to new materials. He was uncertain of accepting the assignment not just because it would take him beyond the materials with which he was familiar, but also because he was psychologically in the dumps from a marriage breakup. He asked the person hiring him if he wanted to reconsider in light of the above circumstances, but he was told "it will either make or break you."[4] Once Kriegler accepted the position, there was no looking back: he became so absorbed in his work that he had little time for a personal life during the remainder of his career at Nortel.

Not long into the new position, he encountered an attitude that challenged him. He discovered through the grapevine that a subordinate had declared to the rest of the staff that Kriegler's appointment was a good thing since he did not know their field of optoelectronics well. The subordinate felt that he and the others could tell Kriegler just about anything and he would not know the difference. This was not a particularly welcome bit of news, but Kriegler chose to let the comments pass for the time being.

At a conference, he came into contact with several experts in the field and got help from them in deciphering some of the finer points of optoelectronics, a main part of which involves the growing of gallium arsenide chips to create the lasers that transmit voice, data, and video traffic over fiber-optic channels. Next, he went over his staff's lab books, as was his managerial right, to fully assess the situation in his shop. His conclusion was that the unit did not have a proper capability to produce optoelectronic devices.

After reaching this decision, Kriegler started talking to the staff about what could be done to make improvements. Owing to similar problems he had earlier encountered in fashioning silicon chips, he was able to bring some of his own insight to the review. He also brought in some of his former associates and staff from the silicon side, persons whose abilities and commitment he could trust. Altogether, these steps led to improvements in the process of fabricating optoelectronic devices, in particular, "an effective method of screening the lasers at an early stage of the manufacturing process to select the reliable ones, thereby greatly reducing the cost of a packaged laser."[5]

In 1979, Kriegler was promoted once again, to director of the Advanced Technology Laboratory in BNR, which was then (after a corporate reorganization) the seat of corporate expertise in integrated circuits, optoelectronics, and fiber-optic transmission equipment. His job would be to participate with general managers and BNR vice presidents in the allocation of the corporate capital budget to research projects. Within months, however, his disinclination to speak the executive language got him into some hot water.

Nortel had just earlier won its first major contract to supply a fiber-optic network—a 1,400-mile long system in the Canadian province of Saskatchewan. A fiber-optic trial in the Canadian province of Manitoba was also planned. To meet the requirements of both projects for fiber-optic cable, Nortel was in the process of constructing manufacturing plants outside of Ottawa and in Saskatchewan (the latter was a condition of winning the contract). To meet the requirements for lasers and other optoelectronic devices, the general manager of Nortel's transmission products line decided that they would be purchased from a Japanese firm.

Just before Kriegler became director of the Advanced Technology Laboratory, he had attended a conference in Japan, where his reputation in the field of microelectronics elicited a warm reception. His hosts took him on tours of areas off the beaten track, including the facilities of the Japanese firm that signed the agreement to supply Nortel with laser devices. A huge production facility was ready to churn out a supply of global proportions. He nevertheless got the impression that it would take some time before they were up and running since there appeared to still be some research problems (such as how to package the lasers) that would entail a delay in transferring designs to manufacturing operations.

Back in Canada, newly appointed to the head of the Advanced Technology Laboratory, Kriegler attended a meeting with the Nortel general manager and BNR vice president overseeing the transmission products line. When the discussion turned to the Saskatchewan project, Kriegler could not hide his doubts about the ability of the Japanese to deliver a reliable product on time, adding that BNR should provide the lasers and related items instead (in offering to supply them, he was rolling the dice because development of the lasers in his lab was still in progress).

Upon hearing Kriegler raise doubts about the Japanese supplier, the general manager exploded. Furious over having his decision questioned, his face grew dark and he angrily attacked Kriegler. "Who the hell are you to question this decision?"[6] he heatedly demanded. Following the dressing down, Kriegler was practically thrown out of the meeting. The next day, he was chastised by the BNR vice president for talking to the general manager in such a way.

Chastened though he was, Kriegler was still worried that the Japanese devices would not be ready in time and that Nortel might fumble the Saskatchewan contract and Manitoba field trial. He therefore decided to proceed on his own. Part of his budget was discretionary and did not require approval from a higher-up, so Kriegler allotted $400,000 (Canadian), or nearly 10 percent of his total budget, to setting up a team of six researchers headed by Dr. George Chik (who later won Nortel's Innovation Award for his developmental work on optical lasers). They had five months, from January to May, before the delivery deadline.

Kriegler informed his immediate superior of what he was doing, and the latter said, "Go ahead, but keep quiet about it."[7] Later, Kriegler told John Roth about the project when the latter came visiting following his appointment to president of BNR. Roth thought that developing the lasers in-house was a good thing. Still, Kriegler had the feeling he could be out on his ear if his devices were not the ones to end up in the project. After all, he was risking nearly half a million dollars, which was a considerable amount of money back then. If it ended up going down the drain, so could Kriegler's career.

Close to the deadline date in May, Kriegler got a call from the manager of the Manitoba field trial telling him that the lasers from Japan were not ready. Attempting to maintain the veil of secrecy, Kriegler did not let on about his lasers, but the field manager somehow knew and asked for a batch. Kriegler finally agreed to supply the lasers on condition that they were recallable for two years because of reliability concerns given the early stage of development. Soon after, he got a call from the Saskatchewan project manager, who informed him that he urgently needed lasers as well. With the cat out of the bag, Kriegler was happy to oblige immediately, but again with the same proviso regarding recallability. None had to be called back, as it turned out.

Following this victory, Kriegler's team shifted to making long wavelength lasers, versions better suited for transmitting over long distances. Around the same time, the general manager of transmission products called a meeting where he acknowledged that the in-house lasers had saved the day and asked how much money was needed to continue development. After obtaining official funding, over 2,200 lasers were shipped in 1981. This was said to be a crucial turning point—the birth of the fiber-optic line that became Nortel's main engine of growth in the late 1990s and 2000s.

While a key turning point in the history of Nortel, it could have been even more monumental if the influx of funds had extended to other components used in fiber-optic systems. A team headed by Josef Straus was working within Nortel on these other components, but insufficient funding prompted them to quit and set up their own company. Renamed JDS Uniphase Inc. after a merger with another company in the 1990s, the market capitalization of this company soared in the late 1990s as the demand for broadband transmission took off. Straus and the other founders became multimillionaires and leaders of a firm considered by many analysts to have a potential as significant as Intel and Microsoft back in the early 1980s.

In 1985, Kriegler was promoted to assistant vice president for Advanced Technology in BNR. He had by this time become aware of some scientific advances that pointed to a second generation of more powerful lasers and other optoelectronic devices. So he set about to raise funds within Nortel for research and development. John Roth, who was president of BNR until 1986, helped Kriegler put together proposals. Immediately following presentations at the senior executive level, Roth would call Kriegler and give him the news—which was nearly all good. Having proven himself earlier on the Saskatchewan project, Kriegler's views and advice now carried weight. He had the trust and respect of the executives who were in a position to provide the funding.

Several good years followed as the research and development program was ramped up. A highlight was the construction of a solid state laboratory at the Ottawa site. It was a huge building—over 20,000 square feet—and cost more than $20 million to construct. Another $20 million was spent on the equipment inside. State-of-the-art facilities do not come cheap.

During this period, scientific advances were parlayed by the Nortel labs into the second-generation product line envisioned by Kriegler. A highlight was the development in 1987 of a gallium arsenide integrated circuit that could switch data at much higher speeds. Another was the design of the first hermetically sealed laser package, which became the industry standard for several years.

But in 1988, the good times started to fade as the transmission products division came under intense review within Nortel. Suffering from poor sales and low margins as Japanese rivals snatched away market share, a decision had to be taken whether to stay in the business. Research and development activities related to transmission products, particularly Kriegler's large-scale initiative, also came under close scrutiny. Still lacking some of the niceties of speaking the executive language, Kriegler did not navigate these tricky shoals as well as he may have wished.

Ultimately, the Nortel board of directors decided to stay in the transmission business on the grounds that fiber-optic networks offered a discontinuity on which Nortel could focus to regain competitive position. While the Japanese built on their advantage in conventional systems, Nortel would build up a forte in the emerging segment of fiber-optic systems. Some of the push would draw on research conducted under Kriegler's program, but key elements such as the optical lasers were slated to be purchased from a Japanese supplier. Kriegler was once again back to a situation faced earlier in the decade: systems design and manufacturing divisions within Nortel had again chosen to buy components from outside suppliers rather than rely on in-house development at BNR.

In late 1989, the FiberWorld vision, offering a complete fiber-optic system, was announced. One goal was to capture the imagination of customers and get them thinking about including Nortel's forthcoming products in their purchasing plans. But near the shipment time, only 25 percent of the lasers from the Japanese supplier were working within the system. This was not so much the fault of the supplier, but more a reflection of the system design parameters not being defined precisely enough. Once again, Kriegler and his staff came to the rescue. They got more precise specifications and molded their in-house lasers to a harmonious fit. Thus, the OC-48 line, the highest-end transmission network then available on the market, was launched with Nortel's own laser components, providing valuable lessons for future developmental work.

The decision to go after the high end of the transmission market was paradoxically both the weakness and the strength of the Nortel strategy to regain market share. In the early 1990s, there was little need for systems of such high capacity, so sales did not live up to the grand billing. Perhaps the move to the high end was less a rational decision to seize a discontinuity than it was simply "in the DNA of Nortel"[8] to seek to build the biggest and most powerful of anything—sometimes a dangerous tendency that can put a company out of tune with the marketplace.

Whatever the case, the weakness turned into a strength toward the end of the 1990s as multimedia traffic from the Internet and other sources escalated on public telephone networks, generating insatiable demand for broadband. Nortel, a well-prepared supplier at the high end, consequently came up a big winner. FiberWorld did eventually materialize, but after the original vision had been nearly forgotten.

During the early 1990s, while Nortel's fiber-optic systems experienced a slow but steady rise in sales, Kriegler found a way to substantially improve time to market for fiber-optic devices. It was seen as one of his more notable achievements. As a press release from Nortel notes: "Dr. Kriegler…pioneered and implemented a concurrent R&D and manufacturing management model to develop and supply optoelectronic devices. As a result of his process re-design, Dr. Kriegler helped reduce development cycles from several years to less than one year…."[9]

What precipitated his concurrent R&D and manufacturing model was a proposal from one of his staff to develop a new kind of chip. Kriegler gave him and his small team some funding, and after a year of work, they established that the devices not only advanced the technology but also made manufacturing easier and cheaper. Having by now a seasoned unit with the best of equipment at their disposal, Kriegler pressured his lab to take on the additional responsibility for churning out hundreds of the new devices in regular production mode.

It took some doing. Several staff refused outright. Kriegler could have banished these rebels but he choose not to. Nor did he have to: enough of the staff had accepted his entreaties to make a go of it. These individuals went along with Kriegler in part because of a basic loyalty that had sprung up as a result of working together over the years. But it was also due to his persuasion: he argued that if they took over the manufacturing, they would have some independence. They could sell their output to the business units of Nortel and would not have to depend upon them for financing. As producers, his team would have more freedom to deploy their research resources; there would be fewer strings attached.

Such was the modus operandi between 1991 and 1994—his team in BNR manufactured and shipped thousands of devices per year at prices that were less than what the business units would have otherwise paid to an outside source. Nevertheless, the prices were still high enough to give Kriegler's group a sufficient profit, which, of course, was kept under wraps. These profits were the source of financing for their preferred research initiatives.

As Kriegler anticipated, combining the two functions of research and production led to synergies that, in turn, led to reductions in overall cost and time cycles. The experience of doing both in the same place generated insights that could be applied to streamlining both processes. These scale economies subsequently played a significant role in allowing Nortel to stay ahead of competition in supplying high-capacity transmission systems during the early 1990s.

For a while, concurrent R&D and manufacturing also played a role in the survival of Kriegler's very own facilities. In 1991, Nortel acquired the British company, STC PLC, which had a distinguished reputation in fiber-optics research (one of the fathers of fiber optics, Charles Kao, achieved his landmark breakthroughs at the company's research lab in Harlow, England).

However, now that there were two fiber-optic research centers in the company, Nortel executives were presented with the question of where to base the company's fiber-optic research.

Serious consideration was given to closing down the Ottawa site. But since it was regularly churning out and testing devices under the concurrent R&D and manufacturing process, they were able to achieve a better product than Harlow. The output of the latter was handicapped by a lower frequency of output and inferior equipment. So Harlow was retained but was redirected to another niche in fiber-optics.

The STC acquisition was nevertheless finally a factor in bringing the heydays to an end. After Jean Monty sold off STC's submarine cable business, there was less work for STC's fiber-optic manufacturing operations in Paignton, UK. This resulted in Kriegler's lab having to ship their devices to the British plant for assembly. They were then shipped back to North America to the customers. It seemed to Kriegler that this was a kind of make-work project.

While this might have been just an irritation, the real blow was to come during the corporate reorganization engineered by John Roth after he was put in charge of North American operations in 1994. Having production of laser and other optoelectronic devices spread across the Canadian and British locations was not seen as the most efficient use of resources. And as production volumes started to climb in response to greater market acceptance of Nortel's optical products, this inefficiency would grow. So a decision was taken to split off manufacturing completely from the Ottawa lab and reassign it to the Paignton facility. The rationale was that it had been set up specifically for manufacturing, whereas the Ottawa site had not been.

Kriegler agreed with the rationalization for the high volume and routinized devices, but he felt less convinced about including the newer, low-volume devices. In any event, in 1995, he accepted a promotion to vice president of technology at BNR, where he assumed responsibility for Nortel's long-term hardware technology program as well as for the external research program. His last position before retiring at the age of sixty-five was vice president of technology strategy at Nortel Advanced Technology, the successor organization to BNR following a corporate reorganization.

In an interview, Kriegler revealed that he "never thought Nortel would do so well."[10] Perhaps it was a function of being up close and seeing all the problems, but he felt that the allocation of resources within the company was often less than perfect as a result of political machinations. Indeed, he found from his experience that Nortel "could not be less political than a political party."[11] He saw what he thought were many missed opportunities go by: research was cut off in favor of an outside source just when the in-house product was months away from fruition. Or research was run in a stop-and-go fashion, which enabled rivals to jump ahead while the program was in downtime.

He attributed the success of Nortel to several key individuals who put their heart and souls into their work and, at times, put their careers on the line going against the grain. They might have been dismissed if their risk-taking had not paid off in results that were valuable to the corporation. These were the people that Donald Chisholm would perhaps have labeled "intelligent subversives." While sometimes a pain to those around them, they are instigators of the kind of change that can help a corporation adapt to turbulent environments.

In the end, Kriegler received recognition for his efforts when Nortel issued a press release on August 14, 1998, announcing that he was being awarded the Nortel Fellow Emeritus designation because:

> He conceived and implemented the optoelectronic and high-speed electronic research programs at Nortel. The laser devices and integrated circuits that resulted— including high power lasers for the OC-48 Transport Node (2.5 gigabit per second) and a gallium arsenide chip set for the OC-192 Transport Node (10 gigabit per second)—have become fundamental enablers of Nortel's high-speed optical communications products.[12]

Fiber-optic systems got going with the invention of the laser at the Bell Labs of AT&T in 1958. The laser, flickering several billion times a second, is able to transmit large quantities of voice, data, and video in semaphore fashion down thin strands of glass fiber. Interest increased in fiber optics when engineers at Corning Inc. found that adding titanium to the fiber helped move the messages faster. After an aborted effort in the early 1960s, Nortel jumped into fiber optics in the 1970s and accelerated its efforts in the early 1980s. In the second half of the 1990s, Nortel surged ahead of other fiber-optic rivals when it came out with the most advanced systems. What were the specific technological advances that gave rise to this end run?

Up to the middle of the 1990s, fiber-optic strands carried just one beam of light. A major step forward came with the commercialization in 1995 of a technique known as dense wavelength division multiplexing (DWDM). In its first incarnation, it allowed a fiber strand to carry eight different colors (or wavelengths) of light. This new technique required eight lasers, one for each color. It also required a multiplexer by which the different colors were separated and passed down the strand. Each color was a new carrier of data, increasing transmission capacity by as many times as there were colors. Pulsing at 2.5 billion times per second, individual colors in the OC-48 systems could each carry 2.5 gigabits of data per second. This was the equivalent of 32,500 voice calls or forty-eight TV channels per second. Therefore, with eight colors, the total capacity of the fiber strand was raised from 2.5 to 20 gigabits per second.

By 1996, Nortel had found a way to increase the speed of the lasers to 10 billion pulses per second, enabling each color to carry 10 gigabits per second (OC-192). This was the equivalent of 130,000 simultaneous voice calls or 192 TV channels. In addition, Nortel found a way to boost the number of colors that could be shot down a glass fiber to forty so that by 1997, the company had a 40-laser DWDM system pumping 400 gigabits per second down every strand of fiber.

In early 1999, Nortel kept ahead of its rivals by bringing out a 160-color DWDM system, elevating the capacity of a single fiber strand to 1.6 trillion bits (terabits) of data per second. At this level, one strand would support 28 million Internet connections or 360,000 simultaneous transmissions of feature-length movies. But Nortel's souped-up version of Moore's Law kicked in once again when, toward the end of 1999, it announced another speed record—this time to 6.4 terabits per second for a single fiber. This latest version is expected to be ready to ship by the end of 2001.

Nortel's decision to raise the capacity of each laser beam in the fiber strand from 2.5 to 10 gigabits was crucial to giving it the lead over its main rival, Lucent. In the early 1990s, both companies had to decide on which of two available options they would focus for increasing the speed of fiber-optic channels.

One was to boost the speed of each laser—that was the path Nortel took. The other option was to push DWDM into splitting the beam in the strand into a greater number of colors— that was the path Lucent took.

As it turned out, Nortel read the market better. Boosting the speed of each laser would pay off if the demand for broadband transmission really took off, because it would be cheaper to scale up if each laser was pulsing at 10 gigabits as opposed to 2.5 gigabits. Thus, the two rivals were placing a bet on the pace at which demand would increase for broadband transmission. To see why, consider that production of a 1.6-terabit system using 10-gigabit lasers requires only 160 pieces of equipment (corresponding to each color of light). A system using 2.5-gigabit lasers would need 640 pieces of equipment to scale up to 1.6 terabits.

So, when demand for broadband did soar, it gave Nortel the advantage in winning virtually all of the long-haul segment in the fiber-optic market in the late 1990s. This dominance showed up not only in a market share of more than three-quarters but also in the number of contracts won. According to one senior Nortel executive, Nortel won thirty-two of the forty contracts tendered for large networks around the world (up to the end of 1999).

John Roth explained how Nortel arrived at its technological edge this way:

> The thing we learned is that doing DWDM at 2.5 gigabits is a cakewalk. Doing it at 10 gigabits is much tougher. This is because you're driving the laser to turn off and on four times faster, which causes the colors to jitter. When that happens, you can't put them as close together. The trick is to design the laser so it does not move around as much. We've learned how to make the laser stable enough to get 160 colors at 10 gigabits.[13]

Yet, the marketing of the 10-gigabit systems had its moments of uncertainty in the early going. Customers did not want them when first offered. But a breakthrough finally occurred with one of the new carriers: Qwest Communications International Inc. To achieve it, Roth and his staff had to make an innovative offer: Nortel would install the 10-gigabit system at the price of the 2.5 gigabit offered by its competitors, with just enough blades to run at the 2.5-gigabit rate. Whenever Qwest needed more capacity, Nortel would do an upgrade and charge for it then. With the uncertainty removed at no extra cost, Qwest management bought in.

Qwest had a forecast of how fast it would grow, and Nortel had a more aggressive forecast of how fast Qwest would grow. Both were blown away. Having an expandable capacity, Qwest was then able to accommodate surging demand much better that if it had a 2.5-gigabit level system. Moreover, because it was able to respond faster, the company scooped up more business than its rivals, gaining valuable market share. This compelled competing carriers to buy 10-gigabit systems in order to keep up, kicking off an avalanche of orders for Nortel.

⌘

The fact that deep in the bowels of the Nortel behemoth are a bunch of engineers who know fiber optics like nobody else has not escaped the attention of competitors. Attempts have been made to lure them away with more attractive rewards, especially those dangled in a systematic and organized campaign waged in 1999 by California-based Optical Networks Inc., a manufacturer of fiber-optic equipment partly owned by Cisco. In an attempt to stem the outflow of talent, Nortel filed for an injunction with the Quebec Superior Court. The injunction was denied, but the court did order the ten employees who left for

Optical Networks not to divulge trade secrets or to woo coworkers still at Nortel.

In late 1998, the core competency in fiber-optic systems was augmented with the $300-million purchase of Cambrian Systems Corp. from Newbridge Networks. Cambrian had no revenue, and some analysts feared the price paid was excessive, but the company's team of 150 had established an expertise in wavelength division multiplexing for transmissions between cities and the Internet trunk. In short, Nortel was acquiring the on-ramps that would provide better access to the Internet from urban areas.

In late 1999, Nortel further added to its strength in fiber optics by acquiring Qtera Corp., a two-year-old start-up firm leading in the development of technology that extends the distance messages can travel unassisted over fiber-optic networks. Given that pulses of a laser beam start to fade after traveling a certain distance, they need to be boosted by signal generators at intervals along the way. Qtera had technology that increased by ten times the distance a signal could travel without such regeneration. This was an especially important development because of the capacity for dramatically lowering costs.

In early 2000, start-up Xros was bought for $3.25 billion in stock. Xros was developing optical switching technology that routes light beams in optical networks with tiny, reflecting mirrors. This new technology was expected to alleviate congestion at network hubs, where switching (as of mid-2000) involved converting light into electrical signals and then back to light. By eliminating this conversion process and doing the switching of light beams directly, Xros technology would considerably speed up, and reduce the cost of, optical switching.

Shortly after the Xros deal, Nortel issued another $1.4 billion in shares to acquire Core Tek, which was developing "tunable" lasers. The latter could be reprogrammed to operate at a range of frequencies. An immediate advantage was that carriers no longer had to carry as large an inventory of lasers since they did not need to have a reserve for each wavelength in a DWDM system. Down the road, with the ability to change frequencies in a fraction of a second, a tunable laser could be used in conjunction with optical switches to quickly route wavelengths from one fiber to another.

❖

Supplementing Nortel's recent acquisitions of optical networking companies was a commitment made in 1999 to invest half a billion dollars to triple its own optical production capabilities by 2001. Furthermore, disparate optical divisions within Nortel will be consolidated into one line of business, named High Performance Optical Components Solutions. This new line will bring together approximately 6,000 Nortel employees who had been spread over facilities in Harlow (UK), Paignton (UK), Ottawa (Canada), and Research Triangle Park (North Carolina). The team will include engineers working on optical components and integrated circuits, technologists designing new manufacturing and processing techniques, scientists exploring new semiconductor materials, and sales staff located in offices around the world. By bringing all of its optical components divisions together under one roof, Nortel hopes to generate synergies and leverage its optical acquisitions more fully.

14

Looking Ahead

Before Gutenberg invented the printing press in the fifteenth century, only a small fraction of the population could read. Just about the only thing on the best-sellers list then was the Bible (of which there were only 300 or so copies in existence). The advent of movable type changed all that. Within forty years, more than 20 million books were in print. Literacy rates soared, and stores of knowledge sprang up in the form of libraries. In time, the dissemination and retention of ideas created a progression in knowledge, providing a basis for the first scientific and industrial revolutions.

The Internet and allied information networks now being built have the potential to spark another scientific and industrial revolution. The process of inquiry and discovery is aided by the vast stores of information accessible at the click of a mouse. The low cost and higher speed of information retrieval greatly enhances the productivity of the learning process, allowing people to acquire more knowledge in less time. Cross-fertilization of ideas is taken to new heights, bringing further synergy to the advancement of knowledge.

On the industrial front, the elimination of intermediary functions by the Internet lowers the costs of commercial trans-actions and enhances overall productivity in the economy. The way business is done is being dramatically reshaped. Much has been made of online consumer purchases of books, computers, and other items, but the real tidal wave will be business-to-business online transactions. According to market researchers, US consumer purchases at Web stores may not hit the trillion-dollar mark until after 2010, whereas US business purchases over the Internet are expected to surpass that mark before the mid-2000s.

✣

Building the information superhighways of the future is a mon-umental infrastructure project of the same order of magnitude as digging of the canal systems in the 1840s, laying down of the railway grids in the 1880s, electrification of communities in the 1920s, or rolling out of the automobile highway networks in the 1950s. Construction of the Internet picked up in the 1990s, and continues to gain momentum into the 2000s as transmission capacity is expanded to keep pace with explod-ing demand, access bottlenecks are fixed, and infrastructure is erected to support a range of utilities such as e-commerce, videoconferencing, integrated messaging, and voice communi-cation over the Web.

There is so much work to be done that the three companies now at the forefront—Nortel Networks, Cisco Systems, and Lucent Technologies—should all enjoy dramatic growth over the decade. One might emerge with a superiority over the others, but the prevailing practice of second sourcing among carriers and other networking firms will ensure that there is enough business to go around for all three. Service providers like to spread their purchases of equipment over several different suppliers as a way of keeping any one from becoming too aggressive in demanding higher prices.

The deregulation of North American telecommunication markets and rapid technological change in the 1990s has created an upheaval in the provision of communication services to consumers. Local and long-distance telephone companies are no longer barred from competing in each other's territory, and cable TV and satellite transmission companies are free to jump in as well. Indeed, virtually any firm or entrepreneur can set up shop and provide services over a new carrier network. This crossing over of firms from other industries, the birthing of start-ups, and the upgrading of legacy networks is creating a tsunami of demand for networking equipment.

The end result is a war zone in which the threesome of Nortel, Cisco, and Lucent play the role of arms merchants supplying all sides of a steadily expanding list of combatants. It is a recipe for boom times for those dealers. There may even be sufficient demand to carry them through general downturns in the economy. About the only risk may be the possibility of overbuilding infrastructure by overestimating demand. Any attenuation in growth rates for the equipment suppliers will be detrimental for their nosebleed market capitalizations, but these construction slowdowns, if they arise, should prove to be transitory once demand catches up and puts more pressure on available capacity.

Foreign telecommunication equipment makers—such as Siemens, Alcatel, and Ericsson—are currently several steps behind the three front-runners. Deregulation of monopolistic telecommunication markets was slower to come in Europe and elsewhere, which delayed the evolution of foreign telecommunication giants to more entrepreneurial and faster-moving cultures. In addition, congestion on the telephone system due to escalating Internet traffic did not present as large a problem as it did in North America, so foreign firms had less of a sense of urgency in preparing for the convergence of data and voice traffic over the Internet and other networks.

⚜

That leaves just three main gladiators in the ring. However, a three-way contest for a project as big as the Internet is an unstable one—that is, it could collapse into a two-way battle if any two of the parties yield to the temptation to join together and split the spoils. Indeed, Cisco has already approached the others about the possibility of forming just such a team, but nothing came of it. A turn of events down the road in the fortunes of one or more of the belligerents could, however, change their mind about such an alliance. The least likely combination would appear to be between Nortel and Lucent as they have a great deal of overlap in product lines. The most likely combination, especially after the spin-off of BCE's stake in Nortel, would appear to be Cisco and Nortel.

The latter scenario would at least seem to be the conclusion to draw from the published interviews of the current chief executives. As part of the battle for mindshare with customers, all three CEOs draw attention to perceived weakness in their opponents at points in their interviews. The verbal cross fire between Cisco's Chambers and Lucent's McGinn, seems to be the most caustic. One of Chambers's more notable expressions of irritation concerned the "Wanted" posters of him put up on

Lucent premises. "McGinn made it personal. He sent a bad message to his employees,"[1] said Chambers.

By comparison, the sparring between Chambers and Nortel's chief executive is gentler. Indeed, the two men are more likely to toss in the ocassional compliment. When Roth was asked by an interviewer if Chambers was good for his word, Roth replied, "I think John is a high-integrity individual, and I think he's true to his word on this."[2] For his part, Chambers flattered the Nortel chief with, "John Roth has done a good job and they have executed well...."[3] But perhaps the most telling detail comes from a reporter who interviewed all three chief executives for a 1999 article. They noted that the heads of Lucent and Cisco directed most of their barbs toward each other, while hardly saying anything about Nortel.

Not to be overlooked is the possibility of one of the lumbering giants at the back of the pack—such as Siemens or Alcatel—reaching ahead with a stunning takeover or alliance with one of the three front-runners. Cisco or Nortel would be the most likely object of their desires, as both have strengths in areas where the Europeans would like to bulk up. Cisco dominates the router market, while Nortel has emerged with a forte in fiber optics. Siemens, nearly twice the size of Nortel in terms of annual revenues, is capable of swallowing or merging with either one. Alcatel, smaller than Siemens but still larger than Nortel, might prefer the latter as a way to fortify its transport systems line.

For now, Cisco, Lucent, and Nortel are fighting on against each other, blocking jabs and trying to land a few punches of their own. No one will likely deliver a knockout blow, and all three appear destined to benefit handsomely from splitting the rich purse. There are plenty of opportunities for all three to flourish. The only real question concerns who will emerge as the leader to exploit, even as lower-ranked contenders. So who is it going to be? Who is going to be the number one Internet infrastructure firm—an Intel or Microsoft for the rest of the 2000s?

⌗

If size matters, Lucent might have an initial edge, with revenues of $38 billion in its fiscal 1999 (ending September 30). Nortel had $21.3 billion in its fiscal 1999 (ending December 31), while Cisco had $12.2 billion in its fiscal 1999 (ending July 31). Size means greater resources with which to wage war. Notably, Lucent easily outspends the others on research and development, allocating $4.5 billion to this important function in fiscal 1999, compared to $3 billion for Nortel and $1.6 billion for Cisco.

However, size may actually not matter in this business. Given how rapidly markets for networking services are changing, agility in responding to evolving customer needs is crucial. Size is of little use if bureaucracies slow the important tasks of market assessment, product innovation, and strategy execution. In fact, size would actually be a liability if much of it were based upon technologies scheduled to become outmoded, as would seem to be case for the circuit-based voice networks supplied by Lucent and Nortel. The latter two corporations therefore need to find new product lines capable of explosive growth in order to maintain an overall corporate growth momentum in line with Cisco, a company that carries little excess baggage in the Old World technologies.

⌗

Nortel appears to have found that explosive new product line: fiber-optic transport systems. The company is currently the leader in this exponentially growing segment. About 75 percent of Internet traffic courses over its optical pipes in North America. In the sizzling high end of 10-gigabit systems, Nortel currently claims a market share close to 90 percent. Nortel's fiber-optic division began 1999 with quarterly revenue growth rates of 50 percent, and rose to triple digits by the last quarter.

The growth pace will remain red hot. "The demand for broadband is insatiable,"[4] says Roth. Telecommunication service providers want more bandwidth to handle the tidal wave of Internet traffic on their networks. Nortel would have grown even faster in 1999 if it had not run up against capacity limits. There is such a hunger for bandwidth that Nortel foresees sales in its fiber-optics line expanding at triple-digit rates for several years.

Lucent is working on catching up to Nortel through in-house research and acquisitions, building further on its core expertise accumulated over the past two decades. Cisco is trying to catch up mainly through acquisitions, taking over fiber-optic companies such as Cerent. Of the two laggards, Cisco looks most likely to be relegated to the rear, if only because it has little history in fiber-optic systems. In addition, the technology of the companies acquired to date by Cisco appears to be trailing the technology of the leaders. For example, the purchase of Cerent in 1999 gave Cisco a 2.5-gigabit system, a level that Nortel had reached a few years earlier.

While its rivals play catch up in developing high-capacity transmission systems, Nortel meanwhile is pushing ahead in developing the ability to provide end-to-end systems. For example, the company is extending its optical networking skills into the metropolitan ring (the connecting area between the Internet trunk and urban networks) with its OPTera Packet Solution acquired from Cambrian. This product is positioned to ride a surge in demand for bandwidth emanating from businesses turning their Web sites into full-fledged e-commerce operations. The OPTera product will speed up access to the Internet by increasing the number of on-ramps, that is, by allocating different wavelengths in a single fiber to individual high-consumption business users.

On the matter of overcoming the drag of outmoded product lines, Lucent and Nortel are not the only ones at risk. Cisco faces these challenges in its own backyard of enterprise data networks. Having issued a challenge to Lucent and Nortel with its New World–Old World vision, Cisco has awakened the two larger companies. Its old rivals in data networking, Ascend and Bay Networks, are now backed by the deep pockets of Lucent and Nortel, and they should be more formidable competitors as a consequence.

But competitive pressures are intensifying in Cisco's home base not only because of Nortel and Lucent but also because of a range of start-up firms with advanced router products. A main challenger in this regard is Juniper Networks. Cisco has a history of recovering nicely whenever it falls behind in the router technology race. Its strength in marketing, which one rival acknowledges as the best marketing team since IBM in the 1970s, is good at maintaining customer loyalty while Cisco comes out with a solution. However, with the company now engaged in fighting battles on additional fronts against bigger rivals, a question arises concerning just how far its resources can be stretched.

Nor is Cisco guaranteed the leading position in the race to provide the new integrated data-voice networks of the corporate world. A trend is arising that could cut into its prospects. Corporations are starting to outsource their in-house networks to common carriers such as AT&T and Bell Canada, where they will be managed as virtual private networks (VPN). The growing complexity of integrated corporate networks makes it more appealing to contract out the operation to a third party: it keeps costs down and allows more enterprise resources to focus on the primary business mission. As such, corporate networks are beginning to drift out of Cisco's sphere in the corporate market into the sphere of national and international carriers, where Lucent and Nortel have held more sway.

Nevertheless, as Chambers states, "Cisco's advantage is that it is going to be an IP packet world."[5] He believes that the inevitable convergence of voice, data, and video traffic over one network will favor his company's core expertise in packet-based data networks. Voice traffic, digitized to the zeros and ones of computer language, will be so easy to carry on a data network that it will likely be moved at no charge as part of a broader package of transporting more demanding media. Meanwhile, telephone network proprietors, increasingly overburdened with Internet traffic, will be forced to convert to packet-based data networks.

The chiefs of Lucent and Nortel acknowledge that convergence means that data networks will win out over voice networks, but they disagree with the assumption that Cisco can extend its domination of the corporate data networking market to the integrated data-voice networks of the future, especially in the case of carrier networks spanning national and international jurisdictions. As Roth says:

> It's one thing to build a small IP network with a few nodes and a couple of desks on it. It's quite a different matter to build an IP network for a nation. The complexity of problems goes up in orders of magnitude every time you double the size of a network... they [Cisco] will encounter engineering and technical problems they've never seen before....[6]

Another issue is quality of service (QOS). IP data networks are still evolving and have not yet attained the reliability and ease of use of voice networks. While it might be acceptable for an overloaded data network to drop an e-mail or similar forms of data transmission, it is less acceptable to interrupt a voice communication or e-commerce transaction in real time. Other QOS issues involve transmission delays in voice and electronic payments.

The inconveniences associated with voice over IP may be acceptable for everyday communications, especially when it is much cheaper than voice over telephone networks (because voice over IP transmits in packet form, it is defined as data and therefore circumvents regulatory tolls in place on voice networks). But this cost advantage could be largely removed with the stroke of a regulator's pen. And the low cost is not a particular advantage in business settings in which quality of transmission usually takes precedence over cost. As Roth likes to say, "Nobody likes to do business with somebody who sounds like Mickey Mouse."[7]

In the early going, Cisco scored some successes with start-up carriers such as Qwest Communications, which were erecting fiber-optic networks from scratch. But in the case of existing carriers with legacy systems, Cisco has not done so well. In fact, in 1999, it lost two high-profile contracts in this segment. The 1998 agreement to supply equipment to Sprint's Integrated On-Demand Network and the deal signed in early 1999 with Sweden's telecommunication company, Telai AB, were both canceled when Cisco failed to meet milestones. The company picking up the business was Nortel.

In time, the QOS issues surrounding IP networks will be straightened out. How quickly the quality problems are resolved will be important in determining which company benefits the most. A quick resolution favors Cisco, but the design and implementation problems encountered by Cisco suggest a period of transition that likely will stretch out over a few years, giving Lucent and Nortel time to respond.

In the meantime, the regional Bell companies and other carriers are wrestling with some serious problems of congestion on their networks arising from rising data traffic from Internet users. For them to abandon their voice networks in which hundreds of billions of dollars have been invested and then spend hundreds of billions more for the still-uncertain performance of all-IP networks, seems too radical a leap. Nortel's solution, which cuts operating and capital costs over 50 percent by redirecting data traffic onto data overlays (while keeping voice traffic on the telephone network) appears to have more appeal at this stage. That way, voice messages retain their reliability and quality. Furthermore, customer call features such as call forwarding do not have to be reinvented.

As mentioned, one way Nortel has differentiated itself from its two main rivals is through its lead in fiber optics. A second differentiation is the greater amount of research and development Nortel is spending on IP networks: over $1.5 billion in fiscal 1999. Lucent's R&D is not concentrated in IP to the same extent. Cisco's total budget is not even as much as what Nortel is spending on IP networks. For customers contemplating which firm to select in helping them build IP networks over the 2000s, more spending in this area is an attractive feature as it signals a greater commitment to staying leading edge.

A third way in which Nortel has set itself apart is through product and geographical diversification. In 1998, before the flurry of acquisitions in the data networking realm, Nortel derived more than 15 percent of its revenues from data network products, far higher than the percentage for Lucent. Thus, when it comes to combining voice and data networks for the converging world, Nortel has more experience with both kinds of networks than Lucent. Cisco has plenty of data networking experience, but its presence in another important product grouping, wireless networks, is rather minimal. On the other hand, over 20 percent of Nortel's sales come from wireless product lines. Therefore, for the building of integrated data-voice networks over wireless networks, Nortel may have a growth opportunity that Cisco does not.

When it comes to serving different geographical markets, Nortel again has more balance. Lucent and Cisco are concentrated in the United States and are hence more vulnerable to an economic downturn in North America. Nortel has significant presence in European and Latin American telecommunication markets, both of which are going through a process of deregulation that is unleashing great growth opportunities. And being more of a global supplier of network systems is a plus when dealing with customers who themselves are global operations.

A fourth way Nortel has differentiated itself is by moving faster than Lucent to embrace the growth opportunities of the Internet and IP networks. The most obvious sign of this was the acquisition of a major data networking firm nearly a year ahead of Lucent. A year in the fast-paced markets of data communication is a long time, giving Nortel an important head start in the melding of data-voice networks.

The data networking firm Lucent bought was Ascend, a company that was focused on ATM networks; Nortel acquired Bay Networks, a company focused on IP networks. ATM was one of the first packet-based technologies that telephone companies felt comfortable using to carry both voice and data. IP technology, although it is not yet as reliable, is capable of handling more voice, data, and video traffic. If Internet traffic continues to soar, networking companies will want to move from ATM to IP as QOS issues are resolved. Once again, Nortel and Lucent have placed a bet on the pace of change: if Internet usage continues to escalate dramatically, it will favor Nortel over Lucent. If it does not, Nortel may still do well because of its existing ATM product line, but Lucent's large investment in ATM might prove to be more lucrative than Nortel's bet on IP.

A fifth way Nortel is distinguishing itself is through the leveraging of its strength in optical transmission. A big question is how to feed those high-capacity pipes being put in place. The answer is with terabit optical routers. Nortel had been working on these large routers with Avici Systems, but cooperation broke off in 1999. Instead, Nortel will continue integrating its own in-house terabit router with the one Bay was designing. Optical terabit routers are much different than the routers made by Cisco for most of its history, so they may be a disruptive technology for the latter.

Cisco's quick adjustment to technological change via a succession of acquisitions and their successful integration into the corporate family was probably the most important strength it had in winning out over Ascend, Bay, and other data-networking rivals during the 1980s and 1990s. Cisco's steadily rising share price could be used not only as currency to easily finance the acquisitions but also as the main instrument in the tricky business of bringing new cultures smoothly into the fold. Few problems arise in attracting and retaining key industry personnel when stock appreciation turns over 2,500 employees—nearly 10 percent of the company workforce—into millionaires. The prospect of becoming rich allays doubts and builds morale like few other measures.

With the adoption of the Webtone vision and a series of acquisitions since, Nortel is now successfully emulating what has been a Cisco forte. In fact, in the early stages, Nortel is doing it better if the extent of stock price appreciation is an indicator. In 1999, aided by sales growth in fiber-optic transport systems, Nortel's equity quadrupled in value, while Cisco's just managed to more than double. Thus, Nortel is not letting Cisco differentiate itself on this important matter, and it is either neutralizing or bettering the formula behind Cisco's earlier supremacy.

❖

In the May 1999 issue of the *Red Herring* magazine, Alex Gove wrote, "After wireless telephony and the Internet, high tech's next great inflection point will be fast wireless Internet service."[8] This is a view shared by many other experts. For example, Nicholas Negroponte, the head of the Media Lab at the Massachusetts Institute of Technology, predicted a few years back that telephone conversations and data transfers delivered by wire would eventually migrate to the airwaves. Nortel's chief executive himself told one reporter in 1999 that he looks "ahead to the day when the majority of voice conversation runs on wireless networks."[9]

Most mobile communication devices now in use are second-generation wireless technology. In the works is a third generation that will give wireless devices broadband transmission capability, and open the door wider to the emergence of the wireless Web. Second-generation wireless devices do allow some access to the Internet, but it is a very rudimentary form without many features such as color graphics and full browser capability. Third-generation wireless, due out by the middle of the 2000s in North America, is expected to give as full access to the Internet as wireline methods.

If the magnitude of spending on research and development is a useful predictor, then Nortel is well placed to become a leader in providing the wireless Internet. For several years, the company has been spending heavily on converting the circuit-based wireless network behind mobile communication devices to an IP network that can easily carry both voice and data traffic. The acquisition of Broadband Networks in late 1997 was an important step forward in those efforts. This significant level of developmental activity has led an independent research firm, the Yankee Group, to name Nortel as having the best positioning for the "IP Mobility World." They said, "Nortel has the clout and the IP goods [and]...we believe Nortel has the edge."[10]

In 2000, Nortel was involved in field trials of wireless IP with a variety of companies. In mid-2000, Nortel won a major contract to be the principal supplier to the third-generation cell phone network that Britain's number-two cell phone operator, British Telecom Cellnet, is planning to put in service in 2002. This was a major breakthrough in a strategically important market. Success in Europe will be a good harbinger of success in North America and other parts of the world that will bring on third-generation wireless services at later dates.

⌗

The telephone network took seventy-five years to reach 50 million subscribers; the Web took only four years to do the same. By 1999, the annual growth rate was 10,000 percent, and over 200 million persons were signed up. By the middle of the 2000s, well over half a billion persons are anticipated to be online, and by the end of the decade, the number will likely be in the billions.

Nortel is one of the firms at the heart of the Internet revolution. Racing to meet the exponential growth in Internet use and bandwidth-hungry applications, Nortel, Cisco, and Lucent will all likely enjoy ample prosperity over the decade. Of the three contestants, however, Nortel's history has perhaps given it the best blend of New World and Old World attributes to surface as the top Internet infrastructure firm.

Nortel faced several crises of survival in its history, starting with the withdrawal of AT&T's technical support in the early 1960s. The latter was a do-or-die situation, and the company came through with flying colors, taking on the much-larger manufacturing arm of AT&T and wrestling away major portions of the North American market for telecommunication equipment. Then, when AT&T used its greater resources to catch up in the late 1980s and early 1990s, Nortel renewed itself and went on to greater heights by shoring up its core market and positioning itself in high-growth segments.

In meeting the challenges of the past four decades, the company has gone through several corporate shake-ups—first under Lobb and Light in the 1970s and then under Stern, Monty, and Roth in the 1990s. These frequent transformations have kept the company lean and focused, a battle-hardened veteran well prepared to deal with turbulence and confrontation. The legacy is an entrenched culture of change and innovation, a very valuable asset to have in an industry rife with discontinuities.

The legacy is also an aggressive spirit. Coverage by the *Wall Street Journal* in the early 1980s of Nortel's contract wins with US regional Bell companies contains frequent references to the "aggressive practices" of the Northern upstart. The same aggressiveness continues into the present, as highlighted in 1999 by the $1-billion contract won in Spain to build an IP carrier network for Jazz Telecom. A senior executive for the latter company said Nortel was chosen over Lucent because Nortel put a design team on the project three months before it was let out, while Lucent wanted commitments up front before its designers went to work.

But the aggressiveness is tempered by a wisdom that comes from long experience in dealing with a succession of opportunities in technologies and markets. Nortel is not a company to put all its eggs into one evangelical vision and attempt to lead customers to the technology of the future. Blended into its vision is a pragmatism of supplying customers with what they need now to get to the future. It is a strategy of both following and leading customer preferences with "evergreen" products and of maintaining a growth momentum by positioning for discontinuities wherever they may be.

In Nortel Networks, the fusion of the Old and New Worlds is a blend between Lucent and Cisco. As such, a company at the heart of the Internet appears destined to become *the* company at the heart of the Internet.

Endnotes

Introduction
[1]David Olive, "Leading the Takeover Parade: Cisco Systems," *Financial Post* (www.nationalpost.com/financialpost.asp), January 26, 2000.

[2]*Financial Post*, August 29, 1998, p. R31.

Chapter 1
[1] Michele Martin, *Hello Central?* Montreal: McGill-Queen's University Press, 1991, Chapter 1.

Chapter 2
[1] Robert Collins, *A Voice From Afar: The History of Telecommunications in Canada*, Toronto: McGraw-Hill Ryerson Ltd., 1977, p. 111.

[2]Ibid., p. 71.

[3]Interview with Cy Peachy (former Nortel executive in 1950s), provided by Gerald Levitch.

Chapter 3

[1]David Thomas, *Knights of the New Technology: The Inside Story of Canada's Computer Elite*, Toronto: Key Porter, 1983, p. 25.

[2]Lawrence Surtees, *Pa Bell: Jean de Grandpre and the Meteoric Rise of Bell Canada Enterprises*, Toronto: Random House, 1992, p. 121.

[3]*The Globe and Mail*, February 19, 1983, p. B10.

[4]Surtees, op cit., p. 123.

[5]*Ottawa Citizen*, October. 5, 1999, p. E16.

[6]Ibid.

[7]Thomas, op cit., p. 25.

[8]Ibid., p. 45.

[9]Surtees, op cit., p. 170.

[10]Ibid., p. 171.

[11]Peter Newman, *NORTEL, Northern Telecom: Past, Present, and Future*, Mississauga: Northern Telecom, 1996, p.42.

[12]Surtees, op cit., p.172.

[13]Newman, op cit., p.49.

[14]Ibid., p.50.

[15]Ibid., p. 65.

[16]Eva Innes, Jim Lyon, and Jim Harris, *The Financial Post Selects the 100 Best Companies to Work For in Canada*, Toronto: Collins, 1986, p.68.

Chapter 4

[1]Bell Northern Research, Telesis Interview with Denis Hall: President of BNR from 1976 to 1981, Telesis, No. 92, p. 12–13.

[2]Tim Jackson, *Inside Intel*, New York: Penguin Putnam Inc., 1998, p. 92.

[3]Tim Jackson, op. cit. p. 90.

Chapter 5

[1]Interview with Ian Craig, former chief marketing officer at Nortel, June 6, 2000.

[2]Interview with Colin Beaumont, former chief engineer at Nortel, March 30, 2000.

[3]Interview with Rudolph Kriegler, former vice president of technology at Nortel, May 25, 2000 and June 5, 2000.

[4]Teddy Boys, Nervous Records Website (www.nervous.co.uk/ted.htm).

[5]Interview with John Roth, CEO of Nortel, June 2, 2000.

[6]Bell Northern Research, "The Arts of the Possible", *Telesis*, No. 98, p. 33.

[7]Ibid.

[8]Ibid.

[9]Ibid.

[10]Munter later won Nortel's Award of Excellence: Innovation for having originated many of the techniques used in Nortel's family of digital central office switches. At the time of his award, he had his name on more patents that any other individual in the company—a total of 32 awarded or pending. Among his patents were designs for the digital circuit that gave telephone users the dial tone, busy signal, and three-way conferencing (see Bell Northern Research, "Frontiers," *Telesis*, No. 92, p. 120).

[11]Interview with Helmuth Krausbar, former manager of DMS hardware project at Nortel, April 26, 2000.

[12]Interview with Peter Cashin, former manager of DMS software project at Nortel, April 11, 2000.

[13]Interview with Colin Beaumont, March 30, 2000.

[14]Ibid.

[15]See Department of Communications, *The Supply of Computer Communications Equipment in Canada*, Ottawa: Government of Canada, 1982, p.19.

[16]Wall Street Journal, Oct. 21, 1978, p.1.

[17]Peter Newman, *NORTEL, Northern Telecom: Past, Present, and Future*, Mississauga: Northern Telecom, 1996, p. 64.

Chapter 6

[1]Robert Babe, *Telecommunications in Canada: Technology, Industry, and Government*, Toronto: University of Toronto Press, 1990, p. 180.

[2]Department of Consumer and Corporate Affairs, *The Effects of Vertical Integration on the Telecommunication Equipment Market in Canada*, Ottawa: Government of Canada, 1976, p.11.

[3]H. Edward English, ed., *Telecommunications for Canada: An Interface of Business and Government*, Toronto: Methuen, 1973.

[4]Department of Consumer and Corporate Affairs, op cit.

[5]Lawrence Surtees, *Pa Bell: Jean de Grandpre and the Meteoric Rise of Bell Canada*, New York: Random House, 1992, p. 203.

[6]Ibid., p.203.

[7]Ibid., p. 205.

[8]Ibid., p.267.

[9]Babe, op cit., p. 193.

[10]Ibid., p. 182.

Chapter 7

[1]Peter Newman, *NORTEL, Northern Telecom: Past, Present, and Future*, Mississauga: Northern Telecom, 1996, p. 66.

[2]Interview with Ian Craig, former chief marketing officer at Nortel, June 6, 2000.

[3]Ibid.

[4]Ibid.

[5]Ibid.

[6]Ibid.

[7]*Financial Post*, April 27, 1996, p. 11.

[8]*The Globe and Mail*, November 4, 1994, p. B1.

[9]*Ibid.*, p. B4.

Chapter 8

[1]*Financial Times of Canada*, March 1, 1989, p. 6.

[2]*Financial Post*, July 30, 1990, p. 7.

[3]Paul G. Stern and Tom Shachtman, *Straight to the Top: Beyond Loyalty, Gamemanship, Mentors, and Other Corporate Myths*, New York: Warner Books, 1990.

[4]*Financial Times of Canada*, Jan. 23, 1989, p. 6.

[5]Ibid.

[6]*Report on Business Magazine*, August, 1989, p. 30.

[7]*Financial Post Magazine*, January, 1993, p. 34.

[8]Ibid., p. 35.

[9]*Business Week*, August 9, 1993, p. 7.

[10]*Financial Post Magazine*, January, 1993, p. 35.

[11]Ibid., p. 34.

[12]Ibid., p.35.

[13]*The Globe and Mail*, January 29, 1993, p. B2.

[14]Ibid., p. B2.

Chapter 9

[1]*Report on Business Magazine*, July, 1997, p.39.

[2]*Canadian Business Magazine*, October, 1993, p. 38.

[3]*Maclean's*, July 12, 1993, p. 33.

[4]*Business Week*, February 15, 1993, p. 27.

[5]*The Globe and Mail*, March 13, 1993, p. B8.

[6]*Maclean's*, July 12, 1993, p. 33.

[7]*Financial Post*, June 28, 1997, p. 8.

[8]Ibid., p. 8.

[9]*Financial Post*, June 28, 1997, p. 8.

[10]*Canadian Business Magazine*, October, 1993, p. 37.

[11]*The Globe and Mail*, September 2, 1993, p. B1.

[12]*The Globe and Mail*, June 14, 1995, p. B1.

[13]Ibid., p. B1.

[14]*Canadian Business Magazine*, October, 1993, p. 42.

[15]*Communications Technology Spectator*, July 10, 1996, p. 141.

[16]*Montreal Gazette*, July 23, 1993, p. D2.

[17]*Financial Post*, Jan 25, 1995, p. 23.

[18]*The Globe and Mail*, Nov. 27, 1996, p. B16.

[19]*Financial Post*, June 28, 1997, p. 8.

Chapter 10

[1]*Report on Business Magazine*, July, 1997, p. 39.

[2]Ibid., p. 46.

[3]*Maclean's*, Nov. 17, 1997, p. 52.

[4]Interview with John Roth, CEO of Nortel, June 2, 2000.

[5]Ibid.

[6]Ibid.

[7]*Maclean's*, November 17, 1997, p. 85.

[8]*The Globe and Mail*, April 21, 1997, p. B1.

[9]*Financial Post*, October 11, 1997, p. 6.

[10]Interview with John Roth, CEO of Nortel, June 2, 2000.

[11]Ibid.

Chapter 11

[1]Vicki Contavespi, "The Internet is What It's All About," *Forbes Digital Tool* (www.forbes.com), March 4, 1999.

[2]Lawrence Surtees, "Nortel's New Vision Calls on the Web," *The Globe and Mail* (www.globetechnology.com), February 25, 1998.

[3]*Canadian Business Magazine*, June 26, 1998, p. 95.

[4]David Olive, "Roth Reinvented Company Faced with Fading Market," *Financial Post* (www.nationalpost.com/financialpost.asp), January, 26, 2000.

[5]Vicki Contavespi, "Nortel Quietly Takes the Lead," *Forbes Digital Tool* (www.forbes.com), March 4, 1999.

[6]L. Ian MacDonald, "Nortel's Worth Weighs in Heavy," *Montreal Gazette* (www.montrealgazette.com), November 19, 1999.

Chapter 12

[1]Lawrence Surtees, "How Nortel Scouts its Acquisitions," *The Globe and Mail*, (www.globetechnology.com), June 7, 2000.

[2]Interview with John Roth, CEO of Nortel June 2, 2000.

[3]Martin LaMonica and Jennifer Jones, "Nortel CEO Drives Voice/Data Convergence," *InfoWorld.com* (www.infoworld.com), January 21, 2000.

[4]*Toronto Star*, May 2, 1997, p. E7.

[5]*Report on Business Magazine*, July, 1997, p. 46.

[6]*Canadian Business Magazine*, June 26, 1998, p. 97.

[7]Ibid., p. 101.

[8]*Red Herring Magazine*, October 19, 1998, p. 88.

[9]Interview transcript provided by John Strimas, vice president of corporate relations, Nortel, March 2, 1998, p. 5.

[10]Ibid., p.6.

[11]Nortel Networks, "Advanced Technology," (internal memo), November 5, 1998.

[12]Francis McInerney, telecommunications analyst with North River Ventures Inc., quoted in Trevor Cole, "The Speed of Light," *The Globe and Mail* (www.globetechnology.com), March 31, 2000.

[13]*The Globe and Mail*, January 3, 1997, p. B4.

Chapter 13

[1]Interviews with Rudolph Kriegler, former vice president of technology at Nortel, May 25,2000 and June 5, 2000.

[2]Ibid.

[3]Ibid.

[4]Ibid.

[5]Rudolph Kriegler, BNR's Advanced Technology Laboratory, Telesis, No. 92, p.68.

[6]Interview with Rudolph Kriegler, May 25, 2000 and June 5, 2000.

[7]Ibid.

[8]Interview with George Smyth, senior vice president at Nortel, May 17, 2000.

[9]Press release from Nortel, Nortel Honours Distinguished Scientist: Dr. Rudolph Kriegler Named Nortel Fellow Emeritus, August 14, 1998.

[10]Interviews with Rudolph Kriegler, May 25, 2000 and June 5, 2000.

[11]Ibid.

[12]Press release from Nortel, op cit.

[13]*Ottawa Citizen*, December 13, 1999, p. D7.

Chapter 14

[1]Peter Elstrom and Andy Reinhardt, "Lucent's Ascent," *BusinessWeek Online* (www.businessweek.com), February 8, 1999.

[2]Richard Brandt, "How Can Nortel Balance Voice Customer Needs with a Data Driven Future?" *Upside Today* (www.upside.com), January 12, 1999.

[3]Mark Evans, "Cisco Head Unfazed By Nortel Threat," *The Globe and Mail* (www.globetechnology.com), November 17, 1999.

[4]John Shinal, "Riding the Light," *Forbes Digital Tool* (www.forbes.com), October 27, 1999.

[5]Fritz Nelson and Art Wittman, "Networking's High Priests Sermonize," *Network Computing* (www.techweb.com), December 27, 1999.

[6]*IVEY Business Journal*, November/December 1999, p. 18.

[7]Nelson and Wittman, op cit.

[8]Alex Gove, "Baby Steps: Wireless Service is Growing Up," *Red Herring Magazine* (www.redherring.com), May 1999.

[9]Interview with John Roth, CEO of Nortel, June 2, 2000.

[10]Nortel Networks press release, "Yankee Group Ranks Nortel Networks No. 1 in Wireless Internet," April 19, 1999, quoting C. Vocars, Yankee Group director.

Index